The Baby and the Drive

The Baby and the Drive presents a new reading of psychoanalytic drive theory, as well as offering clinical tools for early identification of difficulties and intervention with babies and their parents.

This volume demonstrates that the concept of the drive is the crucial factor in early life. The drive is presented as a force with pathways that are established in the newborn's psychic development. Four drive fields are distinguished, which are activated during the first year, and the volume examines the points at which they may encounter difficulties and how these difficulties may be treated. *The Baby and the Drive* explains that access to the drives and their activation orients work with the newborn—an operation at once fundamental and indispensable if researchers accept the existence of a subject in the newborn.

Allowing a new orientation in work with newborns and infants, this volume will be a valuable resource for academics, scholars, and students of Lacanian studies and Lacanian analysis. It will also be of great interest to Lacanian psychologists and Lacanian psychoanalysts in practice and in training.

Marie Couvert is a psychoanalyst and clinical psychologist. She practises at the parent-baby unit of the Clairs Vallons Medical Paediatric Centre (Ottignies, Belgium) and the E. Cavell Medical Center in Brussels; she also has a private practice in Brussels. She teaches at the ISFSC (Higher Institute of Social Education and Communication in Brussels) and runs the graduate Seminar on Infants and Babies at the University of Louvain. She is the author of two books and several book chapters.

The Centre for Freudian Analysis and Research Library

Series Editors:
Anouchka Grose, Darian Leader, Alan Rowan

CFAR was founded in 1985 with the aim of developing Freudian and Lacanian psychoanalysis in the UK. Lacan's rereading and rethinking of Freud had been neglected in the Anglophone world, despite its important implications for the theory and practice of psychoanalysis. Today, this situation is changing, with a lively culture of training groups, seminars, conferences, and publications.

CFAR offers both introductory and advanced courses in psychoanalysis, as well as a clinical training programme in Lacanian psychoanalysis. It can provide access to Lacanian psychoanalysts working in the UK, and has links with Lacanian groups across the world. The CFAR Library aims to make classic Lacanian texts available in English for the first time, as well as publishing original research in the Lacanian field.

OTHER TITLES IN THE SERIES INCLUDE

Obsessional Neurosis
edited by Astrid Gessert

Lacan Reading Joyce
by Colette Soler

The Law of the Mother
An Essay on the Sexual Sinthome
by Geneviève Morel

Hysteria Today
edited by Anouchka Grose

www.cfar.org.uk

https://www.routledge.com/The-Centre-for-Freudian-Analysis-and-Research-Library/book-series/KARNACCFARL

The Baby and the Drive

Lacanian Work with Newborns and Infants

Marie Couvert

Translated by
Lindsay Watson

Routledge
Taylor & Francis Group

LONDON AND NEW YORK

First published 2021
by Routledge
2 Park Square, Milton Park, Abingdon, Oxon OX14 4RN

and by Routledge
605 Third Avenue, New York, NY 10017

Routledge is an imprint of the Taylor & Francis Group, an informa business

© 2021 Marie Couvert

British Library Cataloguing in Publication Data
A catalogue record for this book is available from the British Library

Library of Congress Cataloging-in-Publication Data
A catalog record has been requested for this book

ISBN 13: 978-0-367-67819-7 (hbk)
ISBN 13: 978-0-367-43487-8 (pbk)
ISBN 13: 978-1-003-13297-4 (ebk)

Typeset in Times New Roman
by Taylor & Francis Books

Contents

Acknowledgements

I am grateful to Marie-Christine Laznik for her friendship and for inviting me to work alongside her for a number of years through participating in her seminar. There I have found, and continue to find, an inexhaustible curiosity concerning everything that animates young babies, and also a laboratory for research where clinical creativity and theory are always combined, as well as rigorous teaching, a passion for transmission, and a dedication which have opened up this pathway for me.

My thanks to the Clairs Vallons Medical Paediatric Centre (Ottignies, Belgium) and to the Medical Director, Carine Debuck. Also to the Parent and Baby Unit, and its Head of Unit, Pascale Tielmans, for facilitating clinical work with babies on a daily basis. Their unwavering confidence has always enabled me to work creatively in my practice.

I would like to express my gratitude to the following individuals:

To Manoëlle Descamps, for having put me in charge of the seminar on newborns (FCPE); this offered a space for thinking where theoretical hypotheses could be put to the test in clinical settings.

To Pierre Destrée, who read, re-read and patiently corrected the manuscript.

To Aline Goethals: her close reading of the text, and her questioning, led to stimulating and enlightening discussions which energised my writing.

To Catherine Ferron: her enthusiasm for this work, and her attentive reading, contributed significantly to building a wider readership.

To Anne Joos, for her pertinent observations, and the openings up that they have led to.

To Catherine Martens, for her rigorous and stimulating reading of the text.

I am very grateful to Darian Leader for the interest he has shown in my work. He contacted me as soon as my book was published in French. It is an honour that my book is part of the series of which he is the editor.

I am also very grateful to Lindsay Watson for her fine work translating my book.

And finally, to Marika Bergès-Bounes, for the confidence she placed in me by offering to publish this book.

Introduction

Marie Couvert

What is it that we do when we work clinically with babies? This is by no means a new question, but rather a reiteration of the one at the heart of Lacan's teaching: "What is it that we do when we do analysis?"

In our efforts to define the singularity of clinical work with the very youngest infants, any theories about babies, while they may be instructive, are not adequate compasses with which to orientate ourselves. However, I was struck by the "bolder" idea, as Lacan said, of offering some guidelines of a more "structural"[1] nature.

This led me to seek out the trait which animates individual newborns, the one through which they each make their presence felt in a unique way; in other words, their signature. Fundamentally, this means drawing upon whatever a baby offers: a cry, a look, a movement, or, conversely, the absence of any sound, an averted gaze, a recoiling. Any one of these may contain a knowledge unique to the child, and must be considered as being like a language.[2] In every case there is a trait belonging to the baby, something offered for us to see or hear. From the point of view of the analyst, this constitutes a demand for the supposition of the baby's subjectivity *ab initio*. Such a supposition can be made only under transference. So one has to work with a newborn subject, and not with a subject-to-be or a 'proto-subject', if one is called upon to enter into a transferential relation such as has always constituted the framework of the analytic session.

In my own clinical work, which involves 'failed' encounters between mothers and their babies, I mostly come up against the psychical suffering of the mothers and the response of the tiny babies caught up in the spiral of 'failures' in the exchanges between mother and baby. These babies have mothers who are severely depressed or neglectful. Many of the mothers have been maltreated or neglected as babies themselves; others are at the mercy of real situations which make them feel fragmented or dislocated. So the babies cobble together responses which in each case bear witness to the singularity present in these very young subjects. My position as analyst is always to be open to that. Interpreting babies consists in never giving up on trying to find what it is that animates them.

Whether babies show something manifest here or seem to show nothing, they are always, in a sense, writing. And so with some babies, we must be alert to the different ways of opening out and reading their position.

For example, let us take Aya, aged 7 months, who did nothing but sleep. Her mother, who was profoundly depressed, told me: "When she makes a noise, it gets on my nerves, so I put her over there." Those were her words, and they assigned a place to Aya, not only in the psychical economy of the mother but also very concretely in space. In the field of the mother, Aya was the one who must not 'be noisy' and as soon as she was, she was relegated to a double crib: a Moses basket, which itself was placed on a sofa. This double container constituted the maternal environment in which she seemed to have to spend most of her time. From the point of view of fantasmatic representations, she was undeniably reduced to the status of an object that was too noisy. But what did Aya do? How did she position herself when faced with the maternal injunction to make herself forgotten, to make no sound, to anaesthetise any signs of life? She rose to the challenge! Silent and impassive, she had understood that she must sleep in order to occupy 'perfectly' the only place her mother was capable of giving her, the only one her mother could bear.

Some might say that Aya was a hyper-adapted child, but that would be to exclude the choice made by the subject, and moreover, it would in no way help to orientate the direction of the treatment. Conversely, if one takes the side of the supposition of subjectivity in this baby, one might say that Aya knew that she had to choose sleep as her way of existing and of being able to have any sort of encounter with her mother, and thus sleep was an existential symptom for her. And looking at her more closely, this is where Aya seemed to be most alive, when she rose to the challenge and decided to sleep without batting an eyelid. In some sense, the baby's creation, her lucky invention, was sleep. While the latest research shows that babies have an extraordinary appetite for conversation and are gifted with outstanding relational talents, Aya put all her energy into saying nothing at all, and sleeping. That is how she showed us that she knew a thing or two about her mother, and taught us in this way how she could also do without her. To consider this absence of life in Aya as, paradoxically, the most lively aspect of her, may have been a way of crediting her with a certain knowingness, while at the same time granting her a place as subject.

This presupposes two unavoidable requirements in the field of the analyst. Firstly, in order for silence and hypersomnia to become a production, a sort of act through which something of the subject could be made manifest, and in order for this persistent sleep state to be transformed into a sign and a mode of address, an other had to be put into the place of recipient. Inevitably, this caused a certain wavering in the field of the analyst. But this was the price that had to be paid in order for any evolution to take place where different types of knowing are concerned. In the place of the perfect baby perfectly engaged in the process of exchange, which is what ordinarily animates and inspires those who work with very young children, it was necessary to substitute a baby who had one desire, and was perfectly endowed with the ability to achieve it: not to 'bother' her mother.

The second essential condition concerns how we deal with the little child's productions, what I described earlier as Aya's lucky inventions, which for her were silence and sleep. From this point of view, the means at our disposal to work with what belongs to the baby – what Lacan called *lalangue* – would be to describe a cry, or in this case the absence of any sound, the quality of silence, the depth of breathing, the extensive periods of sleep, the appearance or fading away of movements while she slept, just as one describes the productions of the unconscious. This is how we can treat the symptom without eradicating it, by making it exist and even by glorifying it.

Glorifying the symptom – that might be a different way of looking at these babies. But that is not the whole story: like any 'psychoanalytic experience', analysis with very young children has to have a direction, "failing which it errs".[3]

The way in which work with babies can be directed is through the inscription and the setting in motion of the drives. This is a fundamental and unavoidable operation if one is to take up the wager of subjectivity in newborn babies. In other words, the traits in question which in some way personify the very young subject have to be deciphered as an 'ultra-subjective' way of causing the drives to circulate, or not.

It is the drives, or more accurately, their setting in motion, which will construct the baby's psychical reality. It seems, then, that it is the drives that must absolutely be put in place, in order to give form and relief to the psychical life of the baby.

We shall see that the exploration of this conceptual field will allow us to take up a double wager, the one which has always been prescribed by psychoanalysis. The drives appear to be what determines the emergence of psychical life, and thus of structure: but in addition, if we work on the drives, we may be able to inflect the course of that emergence. The drives thus respond to the double-sided question of psychoanalysis, which is both metapsychological – how is psychical life constructed, and what are the conditions necessary for it to emerge? – and technical: what are the operators in the direction of the treatment and how might the subject be able to change what has determined him?[4]

It is in this context that the drive was elevated to the rank of a fundamental concept, first by Freud and later by Lacan.

This book sets out to give an account of the drive in all its conceptual richness.[5]

This study of the genesis of the concept in the works of Freud and the advances made by Lacan should shed light on the nature of the drive, fundamentally and intrinsically linked to the construction and origins of psychical life. Following on from this, by meticulously working on and exploiting the fields of the drives, we will be able to determine how this set of concepts can operate in clinical work with babies.

Notes

1 J. Lacan, 'The Seminar Book 10, Anxiety' (1962–3), ed. J.-A. Miller, Cambridge, Polity, 2014, p. 217.
2 P. Malengreau, 'Paroles de familles', Quarto, No. 88–89, L'enfant dans la civilisation, December 2006, p. 30.
3 J. Lacan, 'Anxiety', op. cit. p. 244.
4 P. de Georges, La pulsion et ses avatars. Un concept fondamental de la psychologie, Paris, Michèle, 2010, p. 157.
5 It seems essential to approach the subject of the drive from its very genesis. I have imposed this discipline on myself because far too often the theory of the drives is associated with Lacan, without adequate recourse to Freud's discovery.

Part I

The drive and the psychical life of babies

Chapter 1

The drive

A Freudian invention

Marie Couvert

The drive, without any doubt, is Freud's most remarkable invention after that of the unconscious.[1] It is a creation which enables us to account for the conditions linked to the emergence of psychical life. It is, therefore, "infantile in origin" and, as we shall see, "sexual in nature".[2] It is precisely the dimension of sexuality that differentiates the sphere of the drive from that of the instincts.

The hypothesis of the existence of the drive first appeared in Freud's *Project* in which he explored the origins of the psychical apparatus. It appeared as "the impulsion which sustains all psychical activity".[3]

Twenty years later Freud made it a key concept of his *Metapsychology*, a scientific concept which as such was destined to undergo a number of modifications.[4] As we shall see, Lacan took it up and made of it "a fundamental fiction".[5]

Characteristics of the drive and the montage of the drive

We may say that the drive as Freud described it in his early works comes into being with the baby's first cry. For the newborn subject, it comes from within the organism, and there is no escaping from it. Freud refers to the pressure of hunger and thirst which demand to be suppressed by satisfaction, even if the latter comes by way of an external action.[6] From this point of view, he did not yet make a distinction between the drive and need. But what was both absolutely revolutionary and modern was that he said that this would allow the baby to have an initial pivot on which to separate "an outside and an inside".[7] It is unusual to find such assertions in Freud,[8] but there, on this occasion, he points to the baby's capacity to differentiate *a minima* between self and other and to initiate a movement towards the other; and this is confirmed by baby observation as well as other theories concerning babies.

Freud equivocates: he hesitates to consider the self-preservative drives as giving the most comprehensive model of the drive. What it is that he wishes to capture is not the organism, but the body of the living being.

One page further on, when he tackles the characteristics of the drive, we read that the *pressure* of the drive "never operates as a force giving a momentary impact but always as a constant one."[9] This creates tension with, and sits uncomfortably alongside, the notion of needs such as hunger and thirst, which themselves are rhythmic in nature. But that is not all; as early as the *Project*, Freud distinguished between "an urgency which is released along the motor pathway"[10] and an urgency that finds satisfaction only through "a specific action" coming from outside.[11]

At first the human baby is unable to initiate this action; it can only happen, he says, thanks to help from someone else: "It takes place by extraneous help, when the attention of an experienced person is drawn to the child's state by discharge along the path of internal change."[12] The *'Nebenmensch'*[13] of the *Project*, by responding to the baby's cries of distress, through actions and words 'codes or supercodes' the unnameable thing which is at the heart of the baby's primordial dependence.[14] Fundamentally, as J. Champeau put it, "the subject is not self-sufficient, which is why he makes demands".[15] In this way, Freud turned his back on an organicist view based on the model of need and its satisfaction via the reflex arc.

On the contrary, everything happens as if in the intricate connection with the other, one might see the setting in motion of a displacement in which the psychical system would no longer be merely internal to the individual but would be situated between the baby and his or her other. Here we see a pre-figuring of the circuit of the drives as described twenty years later in 'Drives and their Vicissitudes'.

If satisfaction can come only from the outside, then it is surely an invitation to theorise the primordial place of the person who takes care of the baby. And Freud is very precise about this: what constitutes caring for a baby is the "supply of nourishment, proximity of the sexual object"[16]; in other words, an intervention coming from the external world which is of a sexual nature. The drive then undergoes a complete change of direction, it is no longer simply linked to the instincts, but is derived from the sexual, that is to say, the ero-ticisation of a relationship, as we can find already described a year prior to the article on the drives in 'On Narcissism'[17] and later in *An Outline of Psychoanalysis*.[18]

Freud oscillated between need and drive, and later between the self-pre-servative drives and the partial sexual drives, and this oscillation constituted the first tension observed by Lacan, and was to provide the basis for his re-working of the theory of drives.

On reading these texts carefully, one discovers that Freud was caught up in contradictions over and over again, and we may assume that the concept of the drive gave him considerable trouble. It is as if he invites us to accompany him in his tribulations and in the twists and turns of his thinking, which themselves are marked by the very same rigour that we find in his work whenever there was a key concept that needed to be elaborated.

Freud continued his analysis of the characteristics of the drive, and then proceeded to tighten up the concept ontologically, moving from the self-pre-servative drives to the partial sexual drives. As we know, the characteristics of the drive which he retained were four in number: pressure, which we have already mentioned, aim, object and source.

As we shall see, the analysis of these characteristics enabled Freud to set up the partial sexual drives as the paradigm of the drives.

Regarding the *aim* of the drive, Freud writes that it always aims at satis-faction, but he then goes on to assert that "there may yet be different paths leading to the same ultimate aim" including "drives which are inhibited in their aim" while still involving a satisfaction.[19] This is a more or less explicit way of saying that a drive can be satisfied by not being satisfied, or at least that it can be satisfied in ways other than achieving its aim. If we take the further step of translating this operation into clinical terms, and more speci-fically of basing it on clinical work with babies, we can recognise that a hungry baby may be just as satisfied by the mother's words as by her milk, at least for a while. This operation, which has been confirmed experimentally,[20] means that the human infant is a being with a hunger for the symbolic and already has the capacity to sublimate. This is why Freud made sublimation one of the vicissitudes of the drive. But that is not all; through this second characteristic, Freud emphasised the importance of differentiating the drive from need, which always has immediate satisfaction as its aim.

As for the *object*, he tells us that it is "what is most variable about a drive".[21] Obviously one might think once again of the breast, which touches on the register of orality, but Freud is quite explicit that it is not necessarily an external object. "It may equally well be a part of the subject's own body."[22] Indeed any number of babies demonstrate that they are capable of finding satisfaction by sucking their thumb or their hand, which can cause a certain bitterness in the mother who finds she is no longer the exclusive object of satisfaction.

This explanation is quite apt, and opens up the possibility of an inter-pretation other than that of anaclitic object choice, which psychoanalysis repeats over and over again, and which makes the baby seem so lifeless. In fact, the object obtains its status uniquely "in consequence of being peculiarly fitted to make satisfaction possible",[23] and it is through this satisfaction that it achieves its aim. Here we have a radically different perspective as to the place of the object from that which we find so often in psychoanalysis, and which has so little to do with clinical reality. The edifice of Post-Freudian analysis is indeed founded on the idea of the lost object. From this point of view, it is the loss of the object and the efforts made to find it again which constitute access to psychical life and the opening up to the field of the sym-bolic. But this only creates an impasse, in shifting the emphasis away from the absolute precedence of the presence of the object over the absence of the object. Yet the entirety of our clinical work with babies is there to open our eyes to the disasters caused when the object is missing or inadequate.

Access to psychical life depends on the emergence of the drive, intrinsically bound up with the Other[24] in its presence as object. In other words, the re-finding of the object, while it has a logical temporal relation to its loss, is always initially linked back to its presence in the time of the real. This is why Marie-Christine Laznik had to say, "There can be no absence unless there is already a presence."[25]

And if babies, in the oral register, can experience a form of satisfaction by sucking their fingers or hands, this is clearly because it is possible to feel replete other than by feeding on milk, other than in an organic sense, but it is also because it constitutes a renewal of the presence of the experience of satisfaction. So then what would be the function of the object of the drive? In fact, "as far as this object of the drive is concerned, we have to understand it as the object of a function". And "the object of the function is . . . to function",[26] as Bergès tells us.

When this is applied to the oral register, the function of the breast would then be: to make oneself sucked, gobbled, vampirised . . . So what establishes the functioning of orality is on the side of "surplus pleasure". Not in terms of having the object, in this case the breast, but of "circumventing the eternally lacking object".[27] The circle is thus completed, and at the same time, we can see the emergence of the movement of tension of this "circuit-like return",[28] so well observed by Lacan.

Where the source is concerned, Freud tells us that it is initially and always bodily, and this provenance on the basis of the real of the body will be "so decisive" for the drive.[29] This is where Freud hypothesises a link between the somatic source and the psychical representation. Here the drive appears as a "concept on the frontier between the mental and the somatic",[30] like a "conveyor-belt"[31] between body and psyche. And Freud insists that it is because the source of the drive is in the body that it has the power to act on the "life of the soul", in other words, on the construction of the psyche. So what would those sources be that are capable of guaranteeing psychical inscription? They are impossible to know, Freud tells us, other than through their aim. Put another way, the source can only be known through its capacity to obtain satisfaction. At this point, Freud refines his investigation and wonders about the particularities of the sources of the drive, insofar as they have such an impact in terms of psychical action. And he concludes that it is quantity and not quality which achieves the effect of inscription.

Once again, there is a tension within the text, and this did not escape Lacan's attention. As we shall see, he took up this detail, and gave it his own imprint, by giving the source the structure of a rim.[32] For in order to be maintained, quantity has to be contained.

The source, then, would have the same kind of particularity as the object: it would be as variable as the latter, and would depend on the principle of satisfaction in just the same way. The only one of Freud's affirmations which truly characterises the source of the drive is the absolute necessity that it should be anchored in the real of the body. Fundamentally, this is a way of saying that it is essential for there to be an encounter with the real of the baby's body. That is what Freud introduced us to in the *Project*: the invitation to recognise the bodily dimension in the very youngest infants.

We shall also see that exploring the catalogue of characteristics of the drive drawn up by Freud would become Lacan's project. The drive was now presented as a montage of absolutely distinct elements: pressure, object, aim and source.

Outline of a topology of the characteristics of the drive

Examining the characteristics of the drive as defined by Freud is not simply of theoretical interest; it also allows us to set out a topology of the drive.

Let us undertake a preliminary 'decoding' by exploring clinical work with babies in the light of the montage of the four characteristics of the drive. If we are prepared to carry out this exercise, we may easily determine pathologies connected with the pressure, others with the aim, and others still with the source and the object.

Clinical work with babies centred around the pressure of the drive suggests we should include within the dynamics of relations any form of the absence of a lack. Since pressure is a constant force, it insists, in order to maintain this state of pressure, never to be completely suppressed or annulled. To a young woman who asked Freud what she absolutely must do and what she absolutely should not do with her baby, Freud replied, "Do whatever you like, because in any case you will do harm!" In concrete terms, this means that the mother should never respond too perfectly to what she perceives as the demands of her baby. This is what Winnicott meant with his concept of the "good-enough mother".[33] Because mothers who want to do too much good, and who exceed their child's expectations, do not allow the child to make itself heard. Their preoccupation aims at extinguishing the signals emitted by the baby, and indeed those signals will eventually be switched off.

From this point of view, the clinic of the drive is aimed at any kind of disturbance connected with rhythmicity (sleep, feeding, holding . . .). The rhythm is a sequence of scansions based on adequately satisfying experiences of attunement, and which form the basis of anticipation. The mothers who know everything, or those who bend over backwards to be perfect, are at the mercy of imaginary imperatives which force them to prove that they are good mothers at all times. These are the mothers who are called 'all-mothers' or 'phallic mothers'. "If the mother claims to incarnate all the functions of her child (if, according to Lacan's schema, she is on the axis a-a'[34]) what happens? Well, for example the child only sees, hears or speaks through the mother's eyes, ears, or mouth",[35] as Jean Bergès pointed out. For these mothers, the baby can't bear to wait for anything, and they themselves thus have to anticipate in advance all of their child's signals.

For example, Erika's mother told me that as soon as her daughter twitched a finger, she would rush to the cradle, lean over and pick up her darling little baby. Then she would offer her breast, but if the baby turned her head away, even very slightly, she would turn her around again, speaking to her and rocking her. If Erika produced a single sound, she would again offer her the breast. She would watch with joy if the child suckled for an instant, but then when Erika withdrew, perhaps to play with the nipple, she would find herself once again being turned around, and rocked to and fro. Erika would close her eyes, wriggling a bit, maybe wanting to go to sleep. But the mother interpreted this as discomfort, and would rush, full of kindness and concern, to change her nappy. Erika was awake, she was grumpy, so something had to be done quickly. The mother would pick her up again, and put her back to the breast. Erika howled, the mother could bear it no longer, she straightened her up, rocked her, Erika cried, screamed . . . And the mother confessed to me in consternation: "Sometimes I wonder if she's better off when I leave her alone in her cradle . . ."

What Erika teaches us is that the pressure of the drive, that which is trying to make itself heard, cannot be re-absorbed, but demands to be taken up in a circuit, following a certain pathway which is none other than that of the drive itself.

Disturbances centred around the aim of the drive demonstrate another form of the suppression of lack, and are nearly always based on an obliteration of drive by need. With this clinical picture, exchanges between mother and baby take the form of immediate satisfaction, without there being a supposition of any other demand from the baby. That which is satisfied is more on the side of the organic, and this does not open up any pathway for forms of repletion which would be more on the side of the symbolic. The aim becomes the extinguishing of the cry, and, consequently, the extinguishing of the drive.

Julien's mother, without any doubt, had based her actions on a deviation from the aim of the drive. Each time the little boy woke up, and as soon as he started to cry, she would interpret it as an imperious demand to be fed. She would immediately take action, heating up the bottle, and a few seconds later, Julien would find himself with a teat in his mouth, and the liquid would be gushing forth . . . Julien's mother had been deprived of milk as a baby. She remembered, when she was very small, having a dry throat and being terribly thirsty. She recalled being scarcely able to stand, and grabbing glasses that had been left on a low table in the sitting room. She cried as she told me how she had drunk the dregs of alcohol to slake her thirst. That is how this mother had become an alcoholic while she was still a baby who could not yet walk. It was now possible to better understand the importance of this liquid which had been so longed-for, but which failed to appear. But at the same time, the key factor in the dynamics between her and Julien was once again the annihilation of lack. "The essential consequence of this is the exclusion of any third term."[36] For Julien, the hurried arrival of the bottle was designed to annul and cover over any other form of demand. Very soon, he ceased to find any pleasure in the bottle; first he would sulk, and then would refuse it all together. This refusal showed he had an appetite for something other than the purely organic. It showed us that the aim of the drive can never be reduced to a satisfaction in the register of need. And then even when this need is not satisfied, as was the case for Julien's mother, we can observe that the aim of the drive can become intertwined with addiction, or more precisely, we observe the eroticisation of a lack; a lack in the real in the case of the mother, and in Julien's case, the lack of a lack.

Disturbances connected with the source of the drive show the necessity for the baby's body to be reacted to and libidinised. In his *Three Essays on the Theory of Sexuality*, Freud already described the way in which exchanges between the baby and the caregiver were for the former "an unending source of sexual excitation and satisfaction from his erotogenic zones".[37] Because "the person in charge of him, who, after all, is as a rule his mother, herself regards him with feelings that are derived from her own sexual life: she strokes him, kisses him, rocks him and quite clearly treats him as a substitute for a complete sexual object".[38] And Freud emphasises that is the "first and most significant of all sexual relations",[39] that it lasts a lifetime and contributes to the choice of object and to the efforts to re-find "the happiness that has been lost".[40] The ordinary mother thus unwittingly sets up the circuit of this primordial sexuality between herself and her baby.

This was not the case, however, with Niels and his mother; in the encounter with her little boy, she was not able to allow the requisite erotic preoccupation to emerge in herself. This mother, totally preoccupied with her function as nurse, did everything too well! Not for anything in the world would she have omitted to wipe her newborn baby's nose. She washed him carefully, cleaning every crevice, rubbed cream onto his bottom whenever she changed him, and constantly took his temperature. Every four hours she would give him his bottle, watching strictly over his sleep cycles. Everything was measured and administered, but as for any pleasure, that she did not give. She was the care-giving mother, preoccupied with administering whatever was needed to her baby, but something in her resisted becoming too involved. In cases such as this the maternal object and the maternal presence are reduced to a purely operational and instrumental function. The sexuality which ordinarily circulates through care-giving is lacking, and the baby, who makes no mistake about the situation, soon starts to show symptoms of hospitalism.

The clinic of the object leads us to consider the preponderance of presence. It shows the importance of whatever it is that has the effect of an encounter for the baby, and brings us back to the necessity of there being a small other capable of offering satisfaction. It presupposes a "de-completion" of the mother, a gift of herself, at the same time as her insisting that she should not be everything to the child, nor be completely satisfying. When the object is found to be lacking, or when it is presented reduced to its most object-like form, it undermines the security of the presence of the other, that is to say, it has the effect of a primordial encounter.

What is at stake here is each and every aspect of the basic care given to babies, in that they insist on being satisfied, and thus allow the drive to become inscribed. It is a way of saying that from the baby's point of view, what was described in the *Project* has to take place in order for the baby to become engaged in the circuits of the drive. In other words, internal excesses such as pain, hunger or thirst demand to be alleviated or soothed by the presence of a mothering other.

Manu's parents were very young, and had clearly been too deprived themselves to be able to give their baby the minimum care necessary for survival. If Manu cried because he was hungry, he would still have to wait until his parents had finished eating, and sometimes his cries would go unheeded. If he was uncomfortable because he needed changing or putting to bed, he had to wait a very long time, and his parents, who were preoccupied with their arguments or their electronic devices, often failed to respond at all . . . Manu would be left alone in his cradle for long periods, or else he would be carted around in all weathers, day and night. Manu was neglected, he lost weight, his complexion turned grey, and he gradually faded away, presenting symptoms similar to those of Niels. But where Niels suffered from the absence of a symbolic presence, Manu was a baby exposed to lack in the real. So we can see that the clinic of the object insists on two things: the incarnation of the maternal function, and the unavoidable irreducibility of the presence of the object.

Although this may appear a little schematic, I have taken the risk of making the following topological distinction:

The clinic centred on *the pressure and the aim* of the drive is largely *a clinic of excess*, of a too-much in the encounter with the other, while the clinic centred on *the source and the object* generally entails an emphasis on *lack and deprivation*.

Put in this way, the hypothesis of the drive would be presented as a constant force issuing from the real of the body, and demanding satisfaction by introducing something of the Other. The object of this satisfaction would vary, as would the source, and would be "intrinsically linked to the notion of *Lust*".[41] Ultimately, the drive would have no function other than to be "a measure of the demand made upon the mind for work".[42]

So here we have, in essence, the ingredients which would enable Freud to make of the drives "the true motive forces"[43] of development. This is very valuable to us, because it demolishes the whole edifice of the notion of an automatic development, taking place via a succession of stages which occur over time. Later on we will see how Lacan radically redefined this movement, separating the drive definitively from need. Conceived of in this way, the psychical apparatus becomes "what I use to get myself going, taking it from the closest human being, and it exists between them and me, and no longer in me or in them".[44]

On the basis of Freud's contribution, we can still, nonetheless, discern the main knotting points which will structure the development of the drives: the interconnection with the other, the sources of the drives and the establishment of the vicissitudes of the drives.

Drive and *Nebenmensch*[45]

While the drive is born with the baby's first cry, without the presence of an other who receives it that cry fades away and the drive dies out. All of Lacan's early teaching is based on this primacy of the Other. We will see that this maternal other is absolutely primordial. To further our understanding of this, we have already noted how Freud used the terms "extraneous help" (Nebenmensch), "experienced person",[46] and the most famous, "the fellow-human being",[47] thus placing the emphasis on the function as much as on the real person. It is a resolutely modern way of saying that it is not sufficient to be a mother in order to receive and treat the baby's drive-infused cry freighted with the drive. The *Nebenmensch* thus comes to indicate a quality of presence which is not necessarily limited to what we call 'father' or 'mother'; and it was Freud just as much as Lacan who took it upon himself to describe in fine detail the requisite characteristics of this presence.

The only thing is, there is less insistence on the characteristics of the baby which have the power to call the presence of this primordial other into being. They are, however, by no means less important, and we might even say that there are certain specific signs on the part of the baby which are relational vectors. The clinics of autism or of prematurity show very clearly that in the absence of these characteristics in a baby, the capacities of the caregiver will be diminished and will eventually fade away.

Let us take, for example, the now-famous film sequence of a baby two hours after birth. The researcher, Emese Nagy, is beside the cot, and gently raises her index finger, a perfectly useless and gratuitous gesture.[48] But the newborn baby is not indifferent to it, seizes upon it, and reproduces the movement exactly, mirroring that of the researcher. She reiterates the movement, and the baby repeats it once more. The third time, the baby does it again, but because he is showing signs of fatigue, the researcher stops the experiment. However, as she is a clinician who is convinced that the newborn baby has intersubjective capacities to the extent of making it the subject of her thesis, she comes to say goodbye to the baby and to thank him for taking part in her experiment. And then in a completely surprising way, the newborn baby spontaneously lifts his tiny finger, thus inviting her to re-engage in the exchange. This dimension of provocation and initiative on the part of the baby cannot fail to have an effect on the adult who perceives it. In the present case, the baby was to have the power to modify the subject of the researcher's thesis, which would no longer be simply on "intersubjective capacities in the neonate" but "the capacity for intersubjective provocation in the neonate".

There is certainly a discernible element of the drive in the baby, which does not fail to have an effect on the primordial Other. For the adult, it is then always necessary to presuppose its existence in order to enable it to emerge. This capacity to suppose the existence of the drive in the baby and to invest in it is intrinsically linked to the introduction of the sexual in the relation between the baby and the person who takes up the position of *Nebenmensch*.

Just when it is generally accepted that it is important to emphasise the vital link to the other, because of the immaturity and the primordial distress of the newborn, Freud introduces the sexual link. "A mother", he says, "would probably be horrified if she were made aware that all her marks of affection were rousing her child's sexual drive and preparing for its later intensity".[49] Freud makes the mother the one who "is only fulfilling her task in teaching the child to love".[50] We find this written from 1905 onwards, in the *Three Essays*, to which we have already alluded. Twenty years later, he took up an even more radical position in the *Outline*. He was bold enough to describe the breast as "the first erotic object", and the mother as the baby's "first seducer".[51] So one might say that a baby could not exist without being part of a couple, and a sexual couple at that. And there is no doubt that of all the varieties of couples, that of mother and baby constitutes the most primitive. Freud went so far as to make it "the prototype of all later love relations".[52] This is a very Freudian way of inviting us to consider the sexuality at the heart of this odd couple. Lacan did not fail to grasp the dimension of subversion in making the mother the one who initiates her newborn child into sexuality and jouissance.[53] This introduction to primordial jouissance, which Freud situated so well within the maternal function, is what enables the drive to inscribe itself during the first few months of the baby's life.

And this means that the drive is without any doubt caught up in the sexual dimension!

Sources of the drive

We have seen that Freud, in his efforts to delineate the emergence of the drive, distinguished between the self-preservative drives and the sexual drives. "I have proposed", he wrote, "that two groups of such primal drives should be distinguished: the ego or self-preservative drives and the sexual drives".[54] And later, he explained that he has not "met with any argument unfavourable to drawing this contrast between sexual and ego drives".[55] In other words, Freud placed the tasks of the preservation of life – more linked to the instincts – under the aegis of the ego and not of the sexual drive.[56]

By differentiating the sexual drives from the ego drives or the drives of self-preservation, Freud opened up a new pathway, affirming that the self-pre-servative drives are insufficient to account for development.

Freud made this absolutely fundamental separation, and it would be made even more radically by Lacan. It is a way of saying that the newborn human subject is not merely a being of needs, and that the body and the organism are not one and the same thing.

In order to delineate the drive, and to separate it from the need for self-preservation, Freud turned to the partial sexual drives. From 1905 onwards, when he first considered the baby's sexual activity in the *Three Essays*, he mentioned the pleasure of "sucking" conceived of as "a sexual manifesta-tion".[57] "In this connection" he said, "a grasping drive may appear and may manifest itself as a simultaneous rhythmic tugging at the lobes of the ears or a catching hold of some part of another person (as a rule the ear) for the same purpose",[58] i.e. something in the tactile dimension. The observation of very young children led him to recognise the drive to look, which pushes children to become voyeurs and exhibitionists.[59] And Freud also mentions "the fact that children feel a need for a large amount of active muscular exercise and derive extraordinary pleasure from satisfying it".[60]

It is curious that more often than not we only focus on two points in Freud where the partial sexual drives emerge in the baby – the sphere of orality and that of the look – whereas he notes two other fields of the drive which can enlighten us in our clinical work with babies. Alongside orality and the scopic, we should also take into account the sphere of motricity, as shown in the work of Jean Marie Forget,[61] and also the register of touch.[62] In mentioning these two other drives, Freud gives us an indication which is particularly valuable in clinical work with babies. When he questions the nature of pleasure linked to muscular activity, and wonders whether it "itself comprises sexual satisfaction or whether it can become the occasion of sexual excitation",[63] he points out that in situa-tions of romping or wrestling with playmates "apart from general muscular exertion, there is a large amount of contact with the skin of the opponent".[64] Touch would then become superimposed upon and added to motor activity. In other words, Freud explicitly steers us towards the impact the drives have on each other. He argues not only in favour of the multiplicity of sources of the drives, but also of their being intertwined and thus reinforcing one another. This is a fundamental fact which has effects on the direction of the treatment in clin-ical work with babies, because we can see clearly that *the intermodality of the drives acts as a reinforcement of the operation of the inscription of the drives.*[65]

What matters here is to grasp what Freud had observed, that the sources of the drives are multiple and depend on their capacity to set something of the sexual in motion in their circuits. "What distinguishes the drives from one another and endows them with specific qualities is their relation to their somatic sources and to their aims",[66] that is, their capacity for being eroti-cised via certain pathways.

From this point of view, the functions of sucking, seeing, touching and moving would not really have the status of partial drives except on the basis of this possibility of introducing the dimension of the sexual, and of following the pathway which determines their circuits. In other words, that which conditions the partial sexual drives is, on the one hand, the differentiation of the sexual drives from those of self-preservation, and on the other, the future of their vicissitudes which is the consequence of the impossibility of their satisfaction by an object.

However, while Freud separates the field of the drives from the field of needs, it remains the case that from the very beginning he tells us that the sexual drives "are attached to the drives of self-preservation, from which they only gradually become separated . . . A portion of them remains associated with the ego-drives."[67] Freud seems to be struck once again by the primacy of the real of the organism, but let us try to follow him in his thinking. The oral drive is certainly supported by the satisfaction of needs, on condition, as we shall see, that this satisfaction is not an end in itself. Where the specular register is concerned, the idea of the scopic drive being supported by those of self-preservation cannot be entirely disregarded if we consider the absolutely vital necessity for the little human being to be caught up in the prism of the Other's look; for without this, no child could become humanised, or at least development would be thwarted. The same analysis can apply to the drives of touch and motricity, which are not strictly speaking drives of self-preservation, but which precede them, because a baby would not be able to survive for long without being touched, cajoled and cradled.

The tension between the self-preservative and the sexual drives is complex. Freud clearly opposes them, and yet he observes a link between them which creates tension. Fundamentally, we can say that the opposition to which Freud drew attention shows us that the drive is never reducible to need and to self-preservative drives. On the other hand, it may derive from them, and this is how the dimension of the real is taken into account. That is to say, there is a necessity for the real of the baby's body to be recognised and responded to. But that which properly constitutes the experience of the drives is the eroticisation and the gain of pleasure obtained in the satisfaction linked to the primordial Other. *The drive, then, would be created by this introduction of the sexual based on a trait of the baby's taken up by the Other, who finds delight in that trait.*

Vicissitudes of the drives and their circuits

Freud refines his delineation of the partial sexual drives when he explores their vicissitudes. At this point, he links the pleasure of seeing to the pairs 'voyeurism-exhibitionism' and 'sadism-masochism', and he shows how the destiny of the scopic drive is to "turn back on itself", onto one's own body, and to "turn itself around" into its opposite, which would be a motor of development.

Only in 1915, on the basis of his investigation of the vicissitudes of the drives, does Freud discern what is really at stake with the partial drives; and he tells us at the start that they are plural. This is a very valuable insight because *the multiplicity of the vicissitudes of the drives is an argument in favour of the singularity of the development of the subject and thus of treatment on a case-by-case basis.*

The first vicissitude of the drives that he mentions is *sublimation.*[68] Freud decides not to take this any further in this article, but nonetheless he opens up an inaugural and provocative dimension, leading us to think quite differently about the drives. It is a paradoxical idea, an invitation to think of satisfaction in terms of other pathways, and in a rather emphatic manner, he suggests that a drive can be satisfied by not being satisfied. Lacan did not fail to grasp this, and argued that theory of the drive puts the very notion of satisfaction into question: "the function of the drive has for me no other purpose than to put in question what is meant by satisfaction".[69]

The next vicissitude that Freud discusses is repression, giving it such an important place that a whole article would be devoted to it in the '*Metapsychology*'. There is general agreement that the action of repression occurs around the period of latency. However, the fact that it is taken up here as one of the vicissitudes of the drive cannot escape our attention. Besides, Lacan taught us that "one must never read Freud without one's ears cocked. When one reads such things, one really ought to prick up one's ears."[70] For those of us who work clinically with babies, it is clear that he shares the Freudian position that there is a kind of psychical activity which is already operative at a very early age. To make repression one of the vicissitudes of the drives is to situate its action as already being at work in the very earliest development of the psyche. Moreover, there are indications of this in the *Project* when Freud explores the experience of pain. "It is harder to explain the primary defence or repression", he writes, "the fact that a hostile mnemic image is regularly abandoned by its cathexis as soon as possible."[71] So there is a treatment by repression!

We can all agree that such an action is not without its consequences at the level of theory. Because if there is repression, then there is most certainly also "psychical work".

Thus we are obliged to posit the hypothesis of the unconscious in the baby just as much as in the child.

There are two other vicissitudes of the drives which Freud discusses: reversal into the opposite, and the turning round against the subject's own self. By reversal into its opposite, Freud means the turning of activity into passivity. As an example, he takes the scopic drive, already evoked in the pairs exhibitionism-voyeurism and sadism-masochism. He then gives precise examples of the active dimension linked to the movement of looking or of torturing, and the passive one of allowing oneself to be looked at or of being tortured. But what is important here is that Freud locates *a first stage* which is *active* and then *a second stage* which causes a reversal into a *passive* aim. We shall see how these two stages are decisive for the development of the drives.

The fourth and final vicissitude, the turning round against the subject's own self, shows another pathway which, in a certain fashion, follows on from a sublimation by extracting satisfaction from the subject him or herself. What Freud evokes here is the baby's capacity to take their own body as an object of satisfaction. This is in a way the pathway of auto-eroticism, but as Marie-Christine Laznik points out, this is only on condition that the dimension of Eros is included within it.[72] Because "this satisfaction must have been previously experienced in order to have left the need for its repetition".[73]

Then, in an absolutely masterly and innovative fashion, Freud traces a sort of trajectory of the development of the drives based on three pathways: active, passive and reflexive. Using a structural perspective which has always been intrinsic to his thinking, Freud now maps out a veritable *grammar of the drives*. On the basis of the examples already cited, he posits activity as primary, and explains that the activity of looking is always directed at an outside object.

In second position, he places the turning around against the self, which presupposes "Giving up of the object and turning of the scopophilic drive towards a part of the subject's own body", in other words, looking at oneself.[74]

Finally, in third position, Freud places reversal into the opposite, that is to say, the reversal of the activity of looking into a passivity: 'being looked at', and at the same time, he says, there is the installation of a new aim.

This is a very brief summary, and yet the consequences of the new aim that Freud refers to would be decisive. Because the third time conceals within its development the establishment of a new subject, "to whom one displays oneself in order to be looked at by him".[75] Lacan went on to make of this an unavoidable stage in the process of the building of psychical structure.

These three times also punctuate and structure the development of the drive while at the same time opening up absolutely distinct vicissitudes of the drives, as exemplified in the clinic. We shall also see that they prefigure the circuit of the drives as it was later set out by Lacan.

Thus we owe it to Freud to have isolated a concept fundamental to our clinical work with babies, which is also in evidence in every adult case. Through his insistence on giving it the status of a scientific concept, he managed to use his hypothesis to delineate the origins and sources of psychical life, while giving an account of the singularity of the subject. We will see later that Lacan, throughout his re-reading of Freud, remained faithful to the latter's contribution. But he also grappled with the impasses inherent in any system of thought which is a work-in-progress, and developed something which is like an operating concept.

Notes

1 The hypothesis of the existence of the unconscious allows us to account for a specific rationality, linked to our psychical life, in the same way that the hypothesis of the existence of the drive is a response to the question concerning the setting up and construction of that psychical life.

2 P. de Georges, *La pulsion et ses avatars. Un concept fondamental de la psychologie*, op. cit. p. 29.

3 S. Freud, *Project for a Scientific Psychology* (1895), Standard Edition 1, p. 317.

4 S. Freud, 'Drives and their Vicissitudes' (1915), Standard Edition 14, pp. 117–40.

5 J. Lacan, '*The Seminar Book XI, The Four Fundamental Concepts of Psychoanalysis*' (1964), London, Hogarth, 1977, p. 163.

6 S. Freud, 'Drives', op. cit. p. 119.

7 Ibid.

8 This thesis was not always maintained by Freud. In his 'Formulations on the Two Principles of Mental Functioning' (1911), we find the idea that the baby comes very close to realising a psychical system with the mother. This idea is still popular today in the form of the notion of a primordial non-differentiation between them. "The infant – provided one includes with it the care it receives from its mother – does almost realize a psychical system of this kind", Standard Edition 12, p. 220 footnote.

9 S. Freud, 'Drives', op. cit. p. 118.

10 S. Freud, *Project*, op. cit. p. 317.

11 Ibid. p. 318.

12 Ibid. p. 318.

13 *Project*, op. cit. p. 331. The designation *Nebenmensch*, literally 'the closest person', 'the one who is beside you', appears for the first time in the *Project*, and is most often translated as 'fellow being' or even the 'caring other'.

14 P.-H. Castel, 'Le cerveau comme "appareil psychique"'? L'épistémologie de Freud dans ses années de formation, avec quelques enseignements pour les relations entre la psychanalyse et les neurosciences'. *Japanese Journal of the History of Psychiatry*, No. 13, 2009, pp. 13–41.

15 J. Champeau, unpublished seminar, cited by Philippe de Georges, *La Pulsion et ses avatars,* Paris, Michèle, 2010, p. 43.

16 S. Freud, *Project*, op. cit. p. 318.

17 S. Freud, 'On Narcissism' (1914), Standard Edition 14, op. cit. pp. 73–104.

18 S. Freud, *An Outline of Psychoanalysis* (1938), Standard Edition 23, pp. 144–207.

19 S. Freud, 'Drives', op. cit. p. 122.

20 M.-C. Laznik reported on a significant experiment in a lecture given on 28 March 2009 at a conference on work with babies hosted by the ASM 13 Alfred Binet, 'La voix lacté' [literally, 'The Milky Voice', a play on words that loses something in translation: La voie lactée = The Milky Way. Translator's note.] The electrocardiogram of a baby fed with milk from the mother's breast or with words of motherese showed exactly the same trace, bearing witness to the same level of satisfaction linked to repletion.

21 S. Freud, 'Drives', op. cit. p. 122.

22 Ibid. p. 122.

23 Ibid. p. 122.

24 In this context, the Other with a capital O [*l'Autre* with a capital *A* in French] allows the distinction to be made from what Lacan described as the little others. We could say that here the big Other (O) designates the parental function while the little other is its ambassador: father, mother or caregiver.

25 M.-C. Laznik, 'Il n'y a pas d'absence s'il n'y a déjà présence. Du rôle fondateur du regard de l'autre'. *La psychanalyse de l'enfant*, No. 10, 1991, p. 123–37.
26 J. Bergès, G. Balbo, *L'enfant et la psychanalyse: nouvelles perspectives*, Paris, Masson, 1994, p. 94.
27 J. Lacan, '*The Four Fundamental Concepts*', op. cit. p.180.
28 Ibid. p. 179.
29 S. Freud, 'Drives', op. cit. p. 132.
30 Ibid. pp. 121–2.
31 G. Cullere-Crespin, *L'épopée symbolique du nouveau-né*, Toulouse, érès, 2007, p. 57.
32 This rim-structure is perhaps not so far removed from the Freudian hypothesis of 'contact-barriers' as described in the *Project*. What both Freud and Lacan seem to emphasise is the necessity for an excess to be contained.
33 D. W. Winnicott, 'The Theory of the Parent-infant Relationship' (1960), in *The Maturational Processes and the Facilitating Environment*, London, Hogarth, 1965, pp. 37–55.
34 J. Lacan, Schema L, in '*Ecrits*' (1966), Trans. Bruce Fink, New York, Norton, 2006, p. 40.
35 J. Bergès, G. Balbo, *L'enfant et la psychanalyse: nouvelles perspectives*, op. cit. p. 91.
36 J. Bergès, G. Balbo, *L'enfant et la psychanalyse: nouvelles perspectives*, op. cit. p.17.
37 S. Freud, *Three Essays on the Theory of Sexuality*, Standard Edition, 7, pp. 125–243.
38 Ibid. p. 223.
39 Ibid. p. 222.
40 Ibid. p. 222.
41 P. de Georges, *La pulsion et ses avatars*, op. cit. p. 25.
42 S. Freud, *Three Essays*, op. cit. p. 168.
43 Freud, 'Drives', op. cit. p. 120.
44 P.-H. Castel, 'Le cerveau comme "appareil psychique"? L'épistemologie de Freud dans ses années de formation, avec quelques enseignements pour les relations entre la psychanalyse et les neurosciences', *Japanese Journal of the History of Psychiatry*, No. 13, 2009, pp. 13–41.
45 S. Freud, *Project*, op. cit. p. 331.
46 Ibid. p. 318.
47 Ibid. p. 331.
48 E. Nagy, 'Index Finger Movement Imitation by Human Neonates: Motivation, Learning, and Left-hand Preference', *Pediatric Research*, No. 58, 2005, pp. 749–53.
49 S. Freud, *Three Essays*, op. cit. p. 223.
50 Ibid. p. 223.
51 S. Freud, *An Outline*, op. cit. p. 188.
52 Ibid. p. 188.
53 J. Lacan, '*The Seminar Book 17, The Other Side of Psychoanalysis*' (1969–70), ed. J.-A. Miller, New York, Norton, 2007, p. 78.
54 S. Freud, 'Drives', op. cit. p. 124.
55 Ibid. p. 124.
56 Freud makes no concession on this point. He differentiates radically between the two fields, and in another text from the same period, 'On Narcissism', he even uses it to make a distinction that allows us to discern narcissistic pathologies.
57 Freud, *Three Essays*, op. cit. pp. 180–1.
58 Ibid. p. 180.
59 Ibid. p. 192.
60 Ibid. p. 202.
61 On the development of the motor drive, see J. M. Forget, *Les enjeux des pulsions*, Toulouse, érès, 2011, pp. 82–100.

62 This field of the drives is explored in the last chapter of this book.

63 Freud, *Three Essays*, op. cit. p. 202.

64 Ibid. p. 203.

65 This is something that it is vital to take into consideration when working with any form of withdrawal, and all the more so when we are trying to introduce a baby who is at risk of autism into the circuit of the drives.

66 S. Freud, *Three Essays*, op. cit. p. 168.

67 S. Freud, 'Drives', op. cit. p. 126.

68 S. Freud, 'Drives', op. cit. p. 126.

69 J. Lacan, '*The Four Fundamental Concepts*', op. cit. p. 166.

70 Ibid. p. 168.

71 S. Freud, *Project*, op. cit. p. 322.

72 M.-C. Laznik, 'Des psychanalystes qui travaillent en santé publique', *Le bulletin freudien*, No. 34, 'Enfance', 2000, p. 104.

73 S. Freud, *Three Essays*, op. cit. p. 184.

74 S. Freud, 'Drives', op. cit. p. 129.

75 Ibid.

Chapter 2

The theory of the drives

A Lacanian reading of the concept of the drive

Marie Couvert

It was Marie-Christine Laznik who first valorised the concept of the drive, and, with the help of Lacan's reading of Freud, used it in the direction of the treatment in clinical work with babies.[1]

In fact, in the very first lines of 'Drives and their Vicissitudes', Freud wrote that the drive, taken as a basic concept, needed to be rethought.[2] Lacan took up Freud's invitation and, through his re-reading, opened up new pathways which delineated what could constitute an outline of psychical functioning in the newborn, and could even be taken as giving the basis of a structural metapsychology of the baby.

From the *Project* and the '*Papers on Metapsychology*', Lacan extracted a model of the drive which has a structuring effect during the first months of the psychical life of the very young child, and he brought to light, far more effectively than many others, what is at stake for the infant subject.

In basing his work on the Freudian text, but at the same time grasping its tensions and its contradictions, Lacan instigated a major shift in the very concept of the drive.[3] He separated once and for all the drives from the instincts, and constructed a new theory of the drives, which he claimed were "radically anti-biological"[4] and were the vector of the sexual. Nonetheless, as we shall see, his re-reading remained very close to the Freudian text. As de Georges puts it, "far from dismantling the concept, Lacan brought it back to life, restoring it in all its fertile vigour."[5]

He distinguished three registers that must be established during the first year of life. In addition to the oral and the scopic drives, already identified by Freud, he added the invocatory drive, which relates to the question of the voice and vocal exchanges.[6]

But above all he introduced the idea of "failure" of the drives, by conceiving of them as a montage in three stages or times, which can also be undone.[7] In Part II of this book, we shall see that this function of failure is central; it is what causes the compulsion to repeat, and it means that the encounter with the object will always fail. With his re-reading, Lacan not only made significant conceptual advances but he also put at our disposal a new system which allows us to give an account of our clinical work and the direction of the treatment with very small babies.

The drive, a structuring fiction

The drive, however, did not become central until late in Lacan's teaching. In the early years, when the signifier and the unconscious structured like a language had primacy, the drive did not get a good press, and did not find a place in his teaching. But if we look more closely, this was perhaps already a way of delineating it, at least as that which resists and escapes the symbolic order. It was not until the 1960s, with *Seminar XI*, that it was elevated to the rank of a fundamental concept. And it then appears as one of the major concepts, alongside the unconscious, repetition and the transference. Out of the six lectures dedicated to the drive, three are resolutely focussed on the newborn child in order to enable us to grasp the elements and the operations which participate in the emergence of psychical life.[8] And the drive owes this status, precisely, to the fact that it "traced its way in the real."[9] From the baby's point of view, this impact of the real would correspond to what Freud had already mentioned in the *Project* when he described the newborn baby as being prey to internal stimuli. That is to say, it would be through the operation of the drive that a first encounter with the real would be processed.

What Lacan understood by this and tried to theorise is the question of the institution of an order and a logic in the midst of the primitive disorder and chaos characteristic of the inaugural first phase in the life of the newborn baby. He said: "What characterises the start is the sound and fury of the drives and it is a question to understand how something of an order can be constructed from this."[10] With clinical work with babies, this shows the necessity for the engagement of the drives, as well as raising the question of the conditions for their inscription. Newborn babies who are not structured on the basis of the drives, either because they resist and defend themselves, or because the primordial other does not acknowledge that they are there, run the risk of developing in atypical ways.

The drive then appears as something which "presses", "something that has an irrepressible character even through repressions", something which one cannot ignore, and which one cannot do without.[11] And Lacan exhorted us to look out for it in our clinical practice: "one has only to be a child therapist to know the element that constitutes the clinical weight of each of the cases we have to deal with, namely, the drive".[12]

By turning his attention to this very earliest phase in a child's life, and to the portion of the real which insists and thrusts from within, Lacan shed new light on how clinical work with babies could illuminate the direction of the treatment in general.

Because that which pulsates and thrusts from within and which has to be caught up by the sexual is also the real which we knock up against, and which becomes the driving force of every psychoanalytic case.

Let us now see how Lacan, in his reading of the concept of the drive, grappled with the tensions inherent in the Freudian text and how he gave them a particular twist, which both clarified and broadened the concept of the drive.

First twist: the drive is the vector of the sexual

The drive that presides over the very earliest part of human life is not in the organic regsiter, and Lacan, following Freud, demonstrated that it could not be otherwise.

It is the body which sets it in motion, but it is not anything to do with the organic as such. This is the first twist Lacan gave to the concept of the drive. Everything indicates that the drive cannot be assimilated to need. And he invited us to re-examine the Freudian text and the characteristics of the drive, in order to show us that "at the very outset, Freud posits, quite categorically, that there is absolutely no question in *Trieb* of the pressure of a need such as *Hunger* or *Durst*, thirst."[13] It is impossible, he said, simply because the first thing Freud told us is that the drive is a constant force. So, "the constancy of the thrust forbids any assimilation of the drive to a biological function, which always has a rhythm", in other words, a beginning and an end.[14] That deals with the question of the origin of the drive, and takes us firmly away from the biological. We can note here that the most recent research into the activity of the foetus highlights two types of sucking: one for feeding, and the other purely for pleasure. And the first type of sucking to emerge, around the tenth week of gestation, is sucking linked to pleasure.

This discovery might well lead us to question our theoretical certainties, at least those which involve the baby as reconstructed by psychoanalysis, since it seems to suggest a basic structure founded on a pure pleasure principle, in so far as it is detached from any instinctual activity. There would thus be a pure pleasure that would form the vector of the drive. This is what supports the Lacanian re-reading of Freud.

Likewise, Freud went in exactly the same direction, since that is where he placed satisfaction. The aim of the drive, he said, is satisfaction. But he did not hesitate to clarify that sublimation was a form of satisfaction even though it is inhibited in its aim. This would enable Lacan to make his first twist a truly radical one, by assigning to the concept of the drive the function of putting "in question what is meant by satisfaction".[15] He linked this to the analyst's everyday clinical work: the lack of satisfaction which some may find satisfying, or even quite delightful.

> It is clear that those with whom we deal, the patients, are not satisfied, as one says, with what they are. And yet, we know that everything they are, everything they experience, even their symptoms, involve satisfaction. They satisfy something that no doubt runs counter to that with which they might be satisfied, or rather, perhaps, they give satisfaction *to* something. They are not content with their state, but all the same, being

in a state that gives so little content, they are content. The whole question boils down to the following – *what* is contented here?[16]

Put another way, the drive forces us to revisit what we mean by satisfaction. "In any case, if I refer to the drive, it is in so far as it is at the level of the drive that the state of satisfaction is to be rectified."[17] And Lacan highlighted the paradoxical dimension of satisfaction, since it can be satisfied precisely by not being satisfied.

The paradox makes us grasp the complexity of the model, and it creates a tension between the drive and its finality. Because what is at play, and is demanding to be rectified, is linked to something completely other. In this divergence the drive creates with respect to its aim, in this quest for satisfaction which has the peculiarity of being precisely not a quest for complete satisfaction, *we are confronted with the very motor of the drive*. And the fuel for this motor is nothing other than the category of the impossible. This is the quest of the drive, this is what animates it and what maintains it. This category of the impossible, which Lacan also called the category of the Real, is in some sense the product of a primordial failure, a failure which is absolutely inaugural, and upon which the entire dynamic of the drive, and ultimately of demand, is founded. The initial encounter of the newborn child would, then, be with an original fault, which is nothing other than the result of the relation of lack of satisfaction between the drive and its object.

This is continuously demonstrated in clinical work with babies, and specifically where orality is concerned. For example, Ali, a baby boy aged three weeks, was constantly hungry. His mother, who wanted to supply his every need, breast-fed him on demand – in other words, practically all the time. And yet Ali never seemed to be satisfied; he gulped down his mother's milk but never showed any signs of being replete. The mother told me she was doing everything right; but she would so like him to sleep, she'd so love to have some peace! Ah, she said it, it just came out . . . But Ali was not fooled. He responded in his own way; it was not milk he wanted, it was something of her. This is also what Sacha showed, but in a different way. Sacha was hungry, too, so hungry that he could not wait. So he cried, he screamed. And yet when his mother talked to him as she prepared to breast-feed him, I could see Sacha opening his mouth – not to latch on to the nipple, but rather on to the melody coming from his mother. Just like an echo, he responded to her by 'jabbering', which touched me, as it did his mother. Here we can see so clearly how the baby's appetite is not satisfied by having the object, not even the breast, but aims to arouse the appetite in the other. As Lacan put it:

By snatching at its object, the drive learns in a sense that this is precisely not the way it will be satisfied. For if one distinguishes, at the outset of the dialectic of the drive, *Not* from *Bedurfnis*, need from the pressure of the drive – it is precisely because no object of any *Not*, need, can satisfy the drive.[18]

Second twist: the object becomes cause of desire and vector of anxiety

Lacan revisited the function of the *object*, discussed by Freud, removing it definitively from the sphere of needs. The breast, which was in question both for Ali and for Sacha, "in its function as object, is to be revised in its entirety".[19] It is, says Lacan, a sort of "amboceptive object", planted on, implanted in, the mother's body.[20] How are we to understand this unless we conceive of the breast as that which emerges from the two, from the baby just as much as from the mother? Lacan gave a more precise explanation: "In the same way that the placenta forms a unit with the child, there stand, together, child and mamma."[21] At first sight, this does not appear so different from the famous unity of 'nipple-mouth' which has become part of the psychoanalytic tradition which remains faithful to Freud and to the note in 'Formulations on the Two Principles of Mental Functioning'.[22] But Lacan went further: he wanted to give an account of the fact that the object functions structurally both as an object of desire and as a locus of anxiety. If one insists on retaining the unity of 'nipple-mouth', then no account is taken of the dimension of desire. How can we desire something which belongs to us and is at our disposal? Lacan never failed to remind us that desire proceeds along the pathway of lack. And for the same reasons, the unity model takes us no further in explaining how anxiety comes into the equation. The entire clinic of orality shows us that the breast is both the object of desire and the locus of anxiety. It is for this very reason that Lacan invited us to revisit the function of the object.

Many who are not of the Lacanian persuasion have denigrated what Lacan wanted to conceptualise as "object *a*". However, I am going to try to demonstrate its pertinence if one wishes to delineate the emergence of the subject from a structural perspective, and the clinical consequences which ensue. Rather than clinging on to the myth of a unity with the object, Lacan presented the object in its function of division. Thus the object would be divisible, and "so we need to conceive of the cut as lying between the mamma and the maternal organism itself".[23] So the breast "presents itself as something in between the offspring and its mother".[24] This signifies that one can grasp it as well as let go of it. Lacan did not invent anything here, he simply observed. What do we see when we look closely at a baby at the breast? "He detaches himself from the breast, he plays."[25] Lacan's observation was very precise. He reported that the baby,

> After the first experience of cession, whose already subjectified character makes itself tangibly felt with the first signs that flash across his face as he starts, nothing more, to form the expression of surprise, he plays at detaching himself from the breast and taking it up again.[26]

From this observation, Lacan drew a conclusion. The object *a*, the partial and divisible object constituted by the breast in the field of orality, the look in the field of specularity, the voice in the field of invocation and touch in the field of the tactile, becomes that which connects the baby with the other. It is not merely an object to be coveted; it is also, for the mother as much as for the baby, a locus of anxiety. But just a moment! said Lacan, "The locus of the anxiety point does not merge with the locus at which the relation to the object of desire is established."[27]

The breast becomes an object cause of desire because it has the power to connect the mother and the baby, while the locus of anxiety is to be found beyond that which unites the child with the breast. "The anxiety point lies at the level of the mother."[28] "It is in some sense exiled in the Other, because, at the level of the mother, it is suspended from the existence of her organism."[29] How are we to understand that? It seems to me that Lacan was thinking in a quite Kleinian way here. Because that signifies that the locus of anxiety is radically on the side of the Other. For the mother, it would be on the side of the baby, with its voracity and sometimes its strangeness, and this explains why she may feel she is being vampirised, or feels so alienated from the baby, or perhaps so responsible for him or her. From the baby's point of view, anxiety is on the side of mother, as being that which can always elude the child, in the form of lack or absence.

The fact that the breast is a divisible object makes it a matter of indifference to the baby whether it is the breast that is offered, or a bottle or a feeding tube; provided, of course, that there is something of the Other in circulation along with the said breast or bottle or tube. The breast thus becomes an object cause of desire at the same time as it becomes a vector tending towards a locus of anxiety situated in the Other. It is one of the forms of the object a, around which everything is set in motion, and around which we never cease to circle; and at the same time, it is what we will never cease to stumble against. It seems to me that clinical work with premature babies has drawn a great deal from this teaching, because nowadays we can observe caregivers who administer tube-feeding quite differently from the way it was done in the past. Enlightened and orientated by the concept "object a cause of desire",[30] these caregivers take pains to offer a quality of presence which leads them, before and during the feed, to stroke the perioral zone of the baby, while talking to him or her. They arouse in these babies the desire and the pleasure which will provoke salivation and sucking, exactly as reading the menu in a restaurant may make our mouth water. Because "even when you stuff your mouth – the mouth that opens in the register of the drive – it is not the food that satisfies it, it is, as one says, the pleasure of the mouth".[31] And just as we may prolong the pleasure by reading and re-reading the menu, as if eating with our eyes were more delectable than eating what we put in our mouth, the drive will find its satisfaction, not by attaining its object but by "circling around it".[32]

This is how Lacan formulated his theory of the circuit of the drives. What he had in mind was, on the one hand, the primordial failure which prevents any assimilation of the object to the satisfaction of a need; and on the other hand, the different vicissitudes of the drive set out by Freud.

Third twist: the source and the fields of the drive

This led Lacan to explore the *source* as the final characteristic of the drive. If satisfaction cannot be achieved by capturing the object, but rather consists in circling around it, this is because the terrain upon which it does so is precisely what stimulates it. Exactly as it is not just any old menu that makes our mouth water!

The terrain of the drive – and Freud never gave on this notion – is the body. Everything has its origin in the body, and Lacan began by investigating the erogenous zones and their structure characterised by rims. "Why does one speak of the mouth", he asked, "and not of the oesophagus or the stomach?"[33] The mouth, the lips or the teeth are what we speak of in terms of orality. And indeed, the buccal cavity does have a structure involving a rim; but that is not all, it is also something that connects with the other. It is the mouth, the lips or the teeth that reach towards the object. And it will also be the mouth which, by remaining silent or crying out, by drooling or biting, will indicate whether an encounter has taken place, and if so, how it has turned out.

We can observe the same pattern concerning the eye and the voice: we find the same structure, with a rim, and the same type of address to the other. Lacan considered the voice as a partial drive in the baby. This was his own creation, and we shall see how it found confirmation in the clinic. Indeed, babies are not just passively spoken to and about by whoever occupies the place of their primordial other; they are also capable of responding and even of initiating an exchange. And of course, the voice, in its acoustic materiality, constitutes an absolutely determining axis in the direction of the treatment.

But what is there to say about the skin? As we saw, it was mentioned by Freud, but for Lacan it did not feature among the registers of the drive operating during the first year of life. Nonetheless it constitutes an erogenous zone, again with a structure involving a rim, an inside and an outside. In certain societies it is even a privileged locus for exchanges of a much closer nature than those we are used to. So I will add it to our list, on the basis of its being involved in the drive as a source in itself.

Above all, however, what singles out the erogenous zones and what makes them so apt for the establishment of the drives is the sexual quantum that they carry. This is why Freud, in his effort to circumscribe the drive, elaborated the model of the partial drives. As Lacan said of Freud's 1915 paper, "The whole point of the article is to show us that with regard to the biological finality of sexuality, namely, reproduction, the drives, as they present themselves in the process of psychical reality, are partial drives."[34]

The sexual in question here, in so far as it participates in the construction of psychical reality, can be encountered only on the basis of the partial sexual drives. Because the partial drives on the side of the life drives are distinguished by the fact that they operate at the level of the economic principle of pleasure. So they find their source at the level of the body, and more precisely of a libidinised body. As we shall see, this opens new pathways in the direction of the treatment, because more often than not it is a question of battling against the desexualisation or non-sexualisation of a newborn baby.

Fourth twist: the passivisation of the subject

When the baby's body is completely libidinised and eroticised by the person who is in the place of the primordial other, the effect will be to trigger the third time of the drive.[35] And it is at the third time that Lacan operated a twist which has two consequences. Let us recall that Freud linked the third time closely to the advent of a new subject, and even went so far as to make it a condition for this advent. In order to show the emergence of this new subject, Lacan substituted a dimension of passivisation for the Freudian passivity. In other words, the passive aim of being looked at becomes an aim with a passive *activation*, which is *to make oneself looked at.* He added that "what is involved in the drive is making oneself seen. The activity of the drive is concentrated in this *making oneself (se faire)*."[36]

Indeed, *he showed that beneath the apparent passivity was an activity which structured it.* He thus emphasised the action which allowed the position of passivity. The structure of the drive, as he noted, "is really completed only in its reversed form, in its return form, which is the true active drive".[37]

It seems to me that we can read in this the coming into being of the fundamental operation of *alienation* which is "the first essential operation" to ground the subject.[38] Lacan in fact concentrated this operation of the realisation of the subject in the "*vel*".[39] In other words, in the choice of the subject; a choice which condemns him to see himself appear only in the field of the Other.

At this stage where Freudian babies *are looked at*, Lacanian babies *make themselves looked at*, making themselves into subjects by taking an active part in becoming the object of the look of an other. There is no doubt an echo of the dimension of *provocation* in the baby which Colwyn Trevarthen brought to light, and which was taken up in the experiments of Emese Nagy that we discussed earlier.

This movement of *making oneself* was conjugated by Lacan in three registers. Where orality is concerned, which engages the baby and the breast because feeding is sucking, let us say that the oral drive is "to make oneself sucked". For the field of the scopic, it would be "to make oneself looked at". And because Freud left his enumeration of the drives open to new additions,[40] Lacan brought in another one, the invocatory drive, where it is a question of "making oneself heard". And I would add, as the list is by no means exhaustive, "making oneself touched".

The second consequence is linked to the process of the installation of the subject itself, that of "a new subject to whom one shows oneself in order to be looked at" in the course of the third time.

In this process of installation, Lacan encouraged us to distinguish whatever does appear from whatever might equally *not appear*: "Namely, of *ein neues Subjekt*, to be understood as follows – not in the sense that there is already one, namely the subject of the drive, but in that what is new is the appearance of a subject."[41] In this way, the third time becomes the moment and the locus of passivisation in the course of which the baby, in making itself the object of pleasure for the other, manifests itself as a subject at the same time as producing a new subject in the other. When the baby begins actively to join in the exchange around nibbling/sucking, stretching out a foot or pushing out the belly to get it sucked by mother or father, there is an effect on the side of the other. It provokes laughter and pleasure, and this is exactly what the baby is aiming at. At such moments, the baby is the agent of a "surplus of plea-sure", which is often rewarded by laughter from a parent. In doing this, the baby is producing something new which did not exist before. This production is transformational, because the child makes itself into a subject at the same time as producing subjectivity elsewhere. From this moment on, we can be quite sure that there is something of a subject. What is established here is a position radically orientated towards the Other. Laznik translates this opera-tion thus: "My jouissance as a baby is her (the mother's) own jouissance."[42] This echoes Lacan's formulation: "Desire is the desire of the Other."[43]

On the other hand, this production does not just occur automatically, and it is precisely here that Lacan introduces the idea of failure. Nothing, indeed, guarantees the installation of a new subject. We shall see that there are con-ditions for this putting into place, and clinical work with babies shows us what is at stake, most notably our work with cases of autism.

So the drive follows a trajectory which completes its circuit in the field of the Other through the installation of a new subject. The subject is thus "condemned to seeing himself emerge, *in initio*, only in the field of the Other".[44] In fact, that is easily verifiable, because the thriving newborn baby is always suspended from the desire of the Other; we might even say that the baby's desire passes via the desire of the Other.

In Saint Augustine's *Confessions,* we can find a passage which has become very famous, illustrating the relation to the Other. Lacan used Augustine's memory to illustrate the functioning of the logic of desire. What does the passage in question say? "I saw with my own eyes," says Saint Augustine, "and carefully observed a baby consumed by jealousy. He could not yet speak and he could not take his eyes off the bitter spectacle of his foster-brother at the breast without turning pale."[45]

A child, doubtless Augustine himself, looked on enviously as his foster-brother suckled at the wet-nurse's breast. This look contained a dash of bit-terness, and yet this is precisely where Lacan locates the inaugural moment of desire, and from which he extracts its logic. The element of bitterness which overwhelmed little Augustine as he viewed this scene came from the thing he was deprived of, while the other enjoyed it. This only rendered the object more precious, and made the child desirous of enjoying it himself. Fundamentally, what is at stake is less "a vital rivalry than a mental identification", as Lacan emphasised.[46] The logic of desire stems from an identification which guarantees the inscription of the Other and at the same time the putting into place of the phantasy. From this moment on, we can be sure that the baby is orientated towards a structure which involves an engagement with the Other.

Fifth twist: the drive is a montage which can be deconstructed

Conceived of in this way, the drive becomes a "montage by which sexuality participates in psychical life".[47] From this point of view, both Freud and Lacan were eminently subversive. In the creation of psychical reality, sexuality is introduced at the very dawn of life. In other words, sexuality, in the form of the partial drives (the oral, the specular, the invocatory and the cutaneous) is introduced and activated at the very earliest stage. So it is not just a case of insisting on the dimension of the sexual, which is present in the child and is nowadays universally recognised. What is in question is the necessity of the engagement of sexuality for the newborn baby. Lacan emphasised

> That infantile sexuality is not a wandering block of ice snatched from the great ice-bank of adult sexuality . . . In the *Three Essays on the Theory of Sexuality*, Freud was able to posit sexuality as essentially polymorphous, aberrant. The spell of a supposed infantile innocence was broken.[48]

Today, in the light of the theory of the drives, we have to recognise the dimension of the sexual in babies, neonates and even foetuses. So then there is the question of how sexuality is introduced for the infant.

Once again, Lacan read Freud carefully here. He focuses upon the *Three Essays* and the *Outline* where the mother is presented as a primary seductress,[49] the one who teaches the infant how to love,[50] and showed us how she initiates her baby into 'jouissance'. It is a question of

> a dominance of the woman as mother, and as a mother who says, a mother of whom one makes demands, a mother who gives orders, and who thereby establishes the child's dependence . . . She teaches her little one to parade. She carries him towards surplus jouissance, because she, the woman, plunges her roots, like a flower, down into *jouissance* itself.[51]

Hence there is jouissance on the side of the baby just as much as on the side of the parent. There is an eroticisation and a circulation of the sexual. This is where Lacan's model of the montage of the drive is so illuminating.

Freud opened up this pathway by saying that it is the displacement of the drive that counts. Perhaps he was thinking of the different libidinal stages? But Lacan read something quite different into this: the idea of a circuit. If we go back to the Freudian text and to its title, what guides the necessary displacement of the drives can be found on the side of their vicissitudes: *the reversal into the opposite and the turning around against the self.*

But reading Freud carefully, if we examine these two vicissitudes closely we can conclude, with Lacan, that there are in fact three. Because reversal into its opposite consists of two distinct processes: *the reversal of an active drive into a passive mode and a reversal of its content.* And Freud insisted "The two processes, being different in their nature, must be treated separately."[52] Let us try to understand this: the reversal from activity to passivity in fact involves two different moments which are differentiated with respect to their aims. This means that, modelled on the voyeur-exhibitionist pair chosen by Freud to exemplify what is in question here, the active pleasure of looking is reversed into a pleasure with the passive aim of being looked at. And Freud added that he had no doubt that activity precedes passivity.

On the other hand, "reversal of its content" presents a problem, in so far as all that Freud meant here is "the single instance of the transformation of love into hate".[53] Well, love and hate emerge from the life drive. There are two possible readings of this.

At first sight, Freud seemed once again to be caught in the trap of the instincts. And Lacan, working on the question of the vicissitudes of the drives, seemed more Freudian than Freud. He followed Freud's train of thought rigorously, and explained reversal of the content in the light of the aim of the drive, just as Freud elaborated it a couple of pages further on. All of a sudden, this gives us something completely different. If we re-examine the above example, we find the movement of looking in the first stage, in so far as it is activity directed towards an outside object, and this is followed by the reversal into passivity: to be looked at, and the establishment of a new aim: to have made oneself into the object of a look, while at the same time being the subject of this reversal. This means that the content of the drive which is reversed in this way is the object, through "the putting into place of a new subject to whom one shows oneself in order to be looked at". This is the *neues Subjekt* evoked by Freud.

However, there is another possible reading, more complex but also closer to the Freudian text, which deserves our attention. Let us go back to the perplexing question of the reversal of content, with the transformation of love into hate. Certainly it is significant that Freud took the trouble to explain that this process results in two distinct vicissitudes, and named them. And now things become clearer if we take into account the fact that the vicissitudes of the drives are intertwined. Indeed, we know that the first stage of activity is followed by the second stage of turning back onto one's own body, and then there is a transition to the third stage of passivity. The passage from the first to the second stage is crystal clear; the fact that the infant subject tries to find an equivalent to the pleasure gained from the other on his or her own body is explained by the process of displacement and the economic principle of pleasure. On the other hand, what is more difficult to explain is the transition from autoeroticism to the third stage of passivity.

Freud, in a rigorously structural way, puts into question the conditions which will lead the baby to turn away from primary narcissism. And what he proposed is that we should note in this movement an inversion from love to hate. In other words, the infant inverts the love object. The one he or she loves is no longer him or herself; the baby turns away from him or herself in order to make him or herself the object of love for an other. And this turning away takes place in a way that favours passivisation.

This is a knotting which is absolutely crucial in the process of the creation of psychical vicissitudes because it allows us to understand what it is that orientates a subject towards an Other or that which, on the contrary, keeps the subject stuck in narcissism. We find here what will preside over and be the signature of the structural difference in a baby between a neurotic destiny and a more autistic one.[54] This thesis was taken up again and further developed by Freud two years later, in the 'Introductory Lectures'. He now emphasised that what causes "object cathexes" comes from the fact that "the ego was obliged to send out its libido so as not to fall ill".[55] And well before that, in his paper 'On Narcissism', he explained that "we must begin to love in order not to fall ill, and we are bound to fall ill if, in consequence, of frustration, we are unable to love".[56] This reminds us again that babies do love, and turn towards the other in order not to fall ill, and that they fall ill when they are unable to love and move towards the other. Here we can see clearly the difference between an organisation which would remain turned in on the child's own body and one which would turn away from it and orientate itself towards the investment of an object. At the same time, what is also clarified is the way that the life drives are intertwined with the partial sexual drives, as Freud emphasised in Drives and their Vicissitudes in order to delineate two absolutely distinct fields.

Let us now examine the final vicissitude of the drive: *the turning around against the subject's own self.*

The aim would now be found in one's own body in a modality which Freud termed autoerotic. "The autoerotic drives are there from the very first", he wrote.[57] Yet Lacan warned us: autoerotic certainly does not mean that one is indifferent to the other:

> For after all, if there is one thing that cannot be said about the infant it is that he shows no interest in what enters his field of perception. There can be no doubt that there are objects deriving from the earliest period of the neo-natal phase. *Autoerotisch* can in no way mean a lack of interest in them.[58]

One may even say it is the complete opposite, because "there would be no emergence of objects if there were no objects of use to me",[59] Lacan reminded us, quoting Freud. This is the reason why autoerotism is here "the criterion of the emergence and distribution of objects"[60] according to the pleasure principle. The baby can only cause pleasure linked to an object to re-emerge if there has been an initial encounter with the latter.

This point of view is also that of Geneviève Haag, who wondered if

> this capacity to satisfy one's drives on one's own body may not depend on something which has already circulated between the external object and an embryonic Ego doubtless constituted during prenatal life, which would condition the truly autoerotic character and status of the drive.[61]

From this point of view, stage 'one', which signals the movement of the newborn's activity towards the object, would in some way condition the emergence of the other two stages, the autoerotic stage when the baby seeks and reproduces this satisfaction by finding it on his or her own body, and the third stage of passivisation, where the baby puts him or herself into a position to become the object of satisfaction for the other. From then onwards, we see to what extent the drive takes the form (or not) of a circuit. This is to say that the succession of the three stages is not guaranteed in advance. There are certain conditions that allow the circulation of the drives, which have their source in the act. To put it in concrete terms: if the mother is not there for the baby because she is too mad or too sad, or if the baby fails to present any traits that might seduce her because he or she is too persecutory or too disappointing or too fragile, the circulation of the drives may be compromised. It is the very fact that the drive circuit is not already inscribed, that "it doesn't happen automatically" that led Lacan to demonstrate something radical about the vicissitudes of the drives, presenting them as a montage in a circuit, but one which could also be dismantled.

It is also the case that what needs to be put in place may simply not occur and we must be alert to this in the clinic. This is, indeed, the aspect that may constitute a compass for the direction of the treatment. We have to acknowledge that the vicissitudes of the drives described by Freud offer a structuring model. They map out and trace a circuit on the basis of three pathways – active, reflexive and passive – following a very precise trajectory which is finely described in the *Metapsychology*.

Lacan went on to define this circuit as "the trace of the act".[62] *So the drive has a power of action which leaves a trace. And this is how it constructs the baby's psychical life in its relation to the Other. The drive, then, is not a pre-given psychical material, but its trajectory in a circuit is what produces it.*

In this way, Lacan situated the drive at the level of a "headless subjectification".[63] Some Lacanians have adopted this qualification in a rather concrete way, whereas it is intended metaphorically. Because of this, they have continued rather carelessly to neglect this concept, which is nonetheless defined as a fundamental one. Because, in the same manner as the unconscious, the drive can only be an empty object, and it is even a condition of possibility in the Kantian sense: it has to remain empty in order to produce subjectivity. For the same reason, they did not consider it worthwhile to take any interest in babies. And yet clinical work with babies opens up new perspectives in our understanding of psychical structuration. It shows us what needs to be put in place in the process of development, and the importance of certain knotting points.

From this point of view, the three, or even four, registers of the drive, constitute the landmarks which can orientate clinical work with babies according to whether the symptoms are to be found in the field of orality, of specularity, of invocation, or of the cutaneous.

But that is not all: the three times of the circuit are also knotting points, anchoring points which are susceptible to failure. This model of the drives offers us twelve operative landmarks, not only in terms of diagnosis but also in terms of the direction of the treatment, according to whether failures occurred at time one, two or three.

In clinical work with babies, where the body and its manifestations are in the process of being formed, this model of the drives is indispensable. It allows us to illuminate and to decipher what is at stake for a newborn subject, and it gives an orientation to our actions.

Because we can't just do nothing here. Working with babies involves an encounter with their body and the modalities of its inscription in the other. This work can never be reduced to a discourse from the other to its subject. From this point of view, if one were to see the parents without the child, it would create an impasse in the encounter with subjects who are already capable of looking and making themselves looked at, of speaking and making themselves understood, of calling out and making themselves picked up, however young they may be.

Children are born, they are there. It is impossible to imagine that they are not. They are there as an agency conditioning parenthood, and they are the actors right at the heart of the analytic encounter. It is up to us as analysts to learn from them.

Notes

1 M.-C. Laznik, 'Pour une théorie lacanienne de la pulsion', *Le discours psychanalytique*, No. 10, 1993.
2 S. Freud, 'Drives', op. cit. pp. 117–18.
3 M.-C. Laznik, 'Pour une théorie lacanienne de la pulsion', op. cit.
4 P. de Georges, *La pulsion et ses avatars. Un concept fondamental de la psychologie*, op. cit. p. 24.
5 Ibid. p. 100.
6 J. Lacan, '*The Four Fundamental Concepts*', op. cit. p. 195.

7 M.-C. Laznik, 'La théorie lacanienne de la pulsion', *La Célibataire*, No. 4, *Lacan a-t-il fait acte?* 2000, p. 71. On the function of failure, see J. Lacan, '*The Four Fundamental Concepts*', op. cit. p.128.

8 This refers to Lacan's lectures of 6 May, 13 May and 29 May 1964.

9 J. Lacan, '*The Four Fundamental Concepts*', op. cit. p. 163.

10 J. Lacan, '*Le Seminaire Livre 4, La Relation d'Objet*' (1956–7), ed. J.-A. Miller, Paris, Seuil, 1994, p. 65.

11 J. Lacan, '*The Four Fundamental Concepts*', op. cit. p. 162.

12 Ibid.

13 Ibid. p. 164.

14 Ibid. p. 165.

15 Ibid. p. 166.

16 Ibid. p. 166.

17 Ibid.

18 Ibid. p. 167.

19 Ibid. p. 168.

20 J. Lacan, '*Anxiety*', op. cit. p. 234.

21 Ibid.

22 S. Freud, 'Formulations on the Two Principles of Mental Functioning' (1911), Standard Edition, 12, pp. 218–26.

23 J. Lacan, '*Anxiety*', op. cit. p. 234.

24 Ibid.

25 Ibid. p. 327.

26 J. Lacan '*Anxiety*', op. cit. p. 327. In fact, all Lacan does here is to reiterate Freud, who observed that "No one who has seen a baby sinking back satiated from the breast and falling asleep with flushed cheeks and a blissful smile can escape the reflection that this picture persists as a prototype of the expression of sexual satisfaction in later life", *Three Essays*, op. cit. p. 182.

27 J. Lacan, '*Anxiety*', op. cit. p. 234.

28 Ibid. p. 234.

29 Ibid. p. 235, translation modified.

30 J. Lacan, '*The Four Fundamental Concepts*', op. cit. p. 168.

31 Ibid. p. 167.

32 Ibid. p. 168.

33 Ibid. p. 169.

34 Ibid. p. 175.

35 At the first stage, babies turn towards the object of satisfaction; at the second stage, they operate a turning around, in order to find satisfaction on their own body; at the third stage, they make themselves into the object of satisfaction for the other.

36 Ibid. p. 195.

37 Ibid. p. 183.

38 Ibid. p. 194.

39 The translation of the Latin *vel* is "either" with the emphasis on, for example, "either one or the other".

40 Freud indeed wondered "What drives should we suppose there are, and how many? [Perhaps] only primal drives – those which cannot be further dissected - can lay claim to importance. I have proposed that two groups of such primal drives should be distinguished: the ego or self-preservative drives and the sexual drives. . . . This much can be said by way of a general characterization of the sexual drives. They are numerous, emanate from a great variety of organic sources . . .", 'Drives', op. cit. pp. 124–5.

41 J. Lacan, 'The Four Fundamental Concepts', op. cit. p. 178.
42 M.-C. Laznik, 'La théorie lacaninenne de la pulsion', op. cit. p. 71.
43 J. Lacan, 'The Four Fundamental Concepts', op. cit. pp. 182–3.
44 Ibid. p. 210.
45 Saint Augustine, Confessions I, VII.
46 Lacan, 'Les complexes familiaux', in Autres Ecrits, Paris, Seuil, 2001, p. 37.
47 J. Lacan, 'The Four Fundamental Concepts', op. cit. p. 176.
48 Ibid. p. 176.
49 Freud writes that the mother "not only nourishes [the child] but also looks after it and thus arouses in it a number of other physical sensations, pleasurable and unpleasurable", Outline, op. cit. p. 188.
50 S. Freud, Three Essays, op. cit. p. 223.
51 J. Lacan, 'The Seminar 1969–70, Book XVII, The Other Side of Psychoanalysis', op.cit. p. 78, translation modified.
52 S. Freud, 'Drives', op. cit. p. 127.
53 Ibid.
54 Clearly Freud was not speaking of autism here. At this time, the demarcation he made between lack of investment of an object and the turning round against the self referred explicitly to psychosis. But this is because he did not have the nosography of autism at his disposal, since the term 'autism' was only created 12 years later by René Kaës.
55 S. Freud, 'Introductory Lectures on Psychoanalysis', Standard Edition 16, p. 421.
56 S. Freud, 'On Narcissism', op. cit. p. 85.
57 'On Narcissism', op. cit. p. 77.
58 J. Lacan, 'The Four Fundamental Concepts', op. cit. p. 190.
59 Ibid. p. 191.
60 Ibid.
61 G. Haag, 'Sexualité orale et moi corporel', Topique, No. 87, Les resurgences de l'archaïque, 2004, p. 3.
62 J. Lacan, 'The Four Fundamental Concepts', op. cit. p. 170.
63 Ibid. p. 184.

Part II

Fields of the drive in the clinic

Chapter 3

The field of orality

Marie Couvert

It is generally agreed that orality, chronologically, comes first.

But that is not all: "saying that the oral drive is chronologically originative isn't the end of the story, its being structurally originative still needs to be justified", as Lacan reminded us.[1] Furthermore, if we emphasise survival and the function of feeding, we would have to agree that exchanges via the placenta come first. On the other hand, orality is chronologically and structurally at the origin because it is the field in which the primary disjunction of satisfaction occurs. In order to grasp how this first disjunction operates, we need to analyse in depth the oral drive, the drive which brings the baby and the breast together. This bringing together is based on an act on the part of the baby, namely, sucking. Lacan, following Freud, understood this as an original act essential to the baby's survival, because neither of them had access to later discoveries that were made thanks to medical imaging. Indeed, we now know that the function of sucking is initially based on pure pleasure, and not on the satisfaction of a need. In utero, the foetus is involved in oral activity, moving the lips and the tongue without any aim connected with feeding. This is a valuable discovery because it alerts us to a movement without any function other than procuring satisfaction. We can think of this pleasure as being linked to the wave-like movement of the amniotic fluid, to the fullness or emptiness of the buccal cavity, or even to a primal game of presence-absence. So we now need to revisit the concept of oral satisfaction.

Lacan emphasised that "the use of the function of the drive has for me no other purpose than to put in question what is meant by satisfaction".[2] Thus, in the sphere of orality, everything would be based on an experience of pure pleasure, absolutely disconnected from any other end. At the same time,

> the nursling and the breast. This is what all the storm clouds of analytic dramaturgy have amassed around – the origin of the first aggressive drives, of their reflection, even their retention, the source of the most fundamental hitches in the subject's development.[3]

The entire clinic of eating disorders, and subsequently also of addiction, is there to show us that orality is absolutely the primary field in which an initial disjunction of satisfaction is operative. It is thus also at the origin "of all the mishaps, anomalies and disparities that can occur at the level of the structuring of desire".[4]

Lacan observed very precisely that in sucking, it is the lips that function. Indeed, the lips have a rim-like structure, which means they are suitable for containing excitation and becoming erogenous. So between the baby and the breast there is another object – the lips, with their sucking movement. The lips also have the property of being able to open and close, they form a red curtain which can act as a screen in front of the great "theatre of the mouth".[5] If the curtain opens, the scene played out will generally be a pleasant and cheerful one, but if it closes, then one finds oneself witnessing the worst of all tragedies. Crucially, this first movement of opening and latching on contains within itself the possibility of letting go. It is precisely in this locus in the field of orality that we can see a first structural knotting point, which at the same time can be a point of failure. At this juncture there is a possibility of entering, or not, into the field of the drive, and we will see that the modalities of this entry map out and configure the clinic of orality. From this point of view, one might say that there are such things as disorders linked to the opening or the closing of the curtain of the lips. So we have to ask the question of what it is that governs the opening or the closing of the curtain. That is the key to this first time of the drive.

First active time: sucking

We now know that whatever initiates the movements of sucking and animates the lips of the human foetus is linked to pure pleasure. We can thus make the hypothesis that it is the same pleasure which would be the motor of oral activity in its function of feeding. So there is an 'extra' which needs to entwine itself with the process of feeding. This 'extra pleasure' might be the smell, the voice or the look of the maternal other. It really does not matter which; what does matter is that this little 'extra' is present. This is why drinking or eating in themselves do not suffice to establish the installation of the circuit of orality. And indeed, there are thousands of examples of chubby babies who remain unsatisfied, as if they were hungry for something else. Of course this does not invalidate the question of the satisfaction of primary needs, but it alters the emphasis we place upon them, by putting the accent on the active position which the baby may occupy at the first moment of the oral stage. It is so true that a significant number of cases of firmly closed lips are due solely to the fact that someone has not taken the time to wait until the baby was ready to open them. From this point of view, all the accumulated knowledge, and particularly that of the child welfare movement, which has culminated in our time in its 'baby-friendly hospitals' and its propaganda about breast-feeding, only serves to hinder this first time of the opening of the curtain of the lips. The instant they emerge, newborn babies find themselves torn away from the mother's belly, and quite often it is the hand of a stranger which stuffs a breast into the baby's mouth, before the child has had a chance to demand it. Let us just imagine ourselves for a moment arriving in an unknown country, with our eyes just about adjusting to the light, and trying to deal with the new reality which surrounds us, when suddenly, without warning, someone opens our mouth and administers some local dish! Without any doubt we would recoil and close our lips. Why should babies do otherwise?

In the field of orality, then, the active role of babies is initially linked to our own capacity to recognise in them and assign to them a degree of appetency. When the mouth opens, and the lips become activated and make sucking movements, it is a sign that the baby is taking part in the montage of the oral drive, by filling its own mouth with appetency. We are then witnessing "the formidable appetite of a healthy newborn baby to enter into a relationship with the other".[6] The symbolic appetency we can observe in the baby from birth onwards is a sign of the primacy of the symbolic register over the state of need. At the same time, it shows us the place that the primordial other should occupy when these initial exchanges take place. If the response is given only in the field of need, this will be followed by refusals to feed, which will tell us that the baby is demanding to be satisfied in another way. And what the baby is demanding, waiting for, looking out for, even trying to provoke, is to ingest that 'little extra'. The question then is how one can notice and welcome this appetency, or on the contrary, how one can impart some desire to a baby if there is a lack of symbolic appetency.

Well, what does an ordinary mother do at this first stage, in order for the baby to be caught up in the circuit of the drives and the dynamics of desire? Lacan would say that she teaches the baby jouissance. There is, indeed, such a thing as a primordial and necessary jouissance in order for the baby to construct a link with the Other, and it is not a case of a "beyond the pleasure principle" or a "surplus jouissance". In other words, what is operative in the first stage is nothing other than a form of primordial jouissance. Our clinical observations teach us that it is absolutely vital to watch out for, and watch over, this operation.

Failure of the first time

Failures of the first time lead us to look afresh at feeding/eating disorders, and to treat them differently. What has failed, and what we should attend to, is not just whether the baby is sucking or not; we need to keep a sharp eye on whether and how the baby is actively seeking the object. From this point of view, a baby may be opening its mouth, sucking from the breast or the bottle, and even swallowing, but that is no guarantee that the oral stage has been reached.

When we speak of disorders of the oral stage, or disorders of the alimentary canal, we have certain preconceptions about what is good and what is not. For example, if the baby refuses the breast or the bottle, we are likely to say, "That's no good". "It's not good" not to latch on to the breast or take the formula we have prepared so carefully. That baby soon becomes a 'bad' baby. Declining to open his or her mouth, refusing to eat, it's not what we expect, it absolutely won't do, and you often hear the caregivers of these babies saying they "haven't a clue what to do", or the parents saying, "He's so naughty!"

But what is eclipsed here, and which constitutes the well-spring of the field of orality, is the extra pleasure required for the active role of the baby. Because the baby has other ideas. If we just allow ourselves to be taught, we will soon learn to understand these refusals to feed in quite a different way. Turning the mouth away, pursing the lips, spitting out food, even regurgitating it, or on the contrary, allowing oneself to be stuffed, or never being full, become individual responses in babies when they are caught up in exchanges of feeding and being fed devoid of the 'seasoning' of this little extra bit of pleasure. Feeding disorders could then be understood as a vital clue, a made-to-measure creation of the baby-subject, a way of biting into, or not, the circuit of the oral drive.

When the curtain of the lips opens, but nothing is being staged in the theatre of the mouth . . . Fanny, a three-month-old baby, taught me that it is quite possible to open one's mouth, to start making sucking movements and swallowing, without having entered the oral stage.

Fanny was three months old when her mother brought her to see me for the first time. Fanny was one of those babies who cry inconsolably – nothing could appease her. She had not stopped crying since she was three or four weeks old. "She really cries a lot," said her mother, who never stopped giving herself reasons why. First of all she convinced herself it was normal – babies, well, they just do cry a lot. Then she thought it was colic, because it was worse in the evenings . . .

The mother was sitting facing me. She had placed the baby seat beside her, so that I could see Fanny, who was asleep; her mother, however, could not see her. In front of me was a fine baby girl, with delicate features; her eyes were closed, and the rhythm of her breathing was slow. I did not notice her moving much while she was asleep; she appeared well, although not totally at ease. Occasionally during the session she would open a heavy eyelid, as if to show me that she was well aware of what was going on. Fanny slept through the whole of the first session, without waking or crying!

The mother told me she had tried everything. If Fanny cried, she picked her up. But as soon as she put her down, she would cry even more loudly. She now found she had to carry the baby around all the time, and this made her older daughter cry as well. And to the extent, she added, that she had to wait until the older child was in bed before she could breast-feed Fanny.

So I now knew that Fanny was the second child, and that she had a sister two-and-a-half years older. The mother continued, admitting that because Fanny never left her arms, they slept together at night, with the baby latched on to her breast. Her friends and family told her that it was just normal 'evening crying', or maybe colic. She became anxious, and days went by without her ever having had a quiet evening. She compared Fanny with the older girl, who had always gone to sleep very quickly as soon as she was put to bed. In those days, she used to be able to go out, she used to be able to leave her daughter with a baby-sitter. With Fanny, none of that had been possible. And then she almost shouted at me, "It's three months, and she hasn't stopped crying. She's making us go deaf! I can't enjoy anything any more!" [Translator's note: "*Je ne profite plus de rien*", *profiter de* entails the ideas of being unable to make use of, take advantage of, or enjoy something.] And she added, "The minute I got the appointment with you, I made an appointment with the osteopath and with the paediatrician. It's as if I was saying, 'Stop, stop, stop'. It can't go on like this!"

I was listening to this young mother, who seemed to be driven by serious maternal concerns, without being able to pinpoint what had failed. Then I heard her say, "OK, she cries a lot, but maybe it's because she can't stand me crying?"

Initially, I had grasped only the meaning implicit in this question of hers: a question about her own capacity to bear her baby's crying, or even her own inability to tolerate it. It was only retroactively, and because I also picked up on her repeated use of the imperfect tense [Translator's note: e.g. see above – "she used to be able to . . ."], that I was able to identify that the way she expressed herself revealed something of her unconscious: her own internal crying.

What is more, the mother came out with a litany of complaints:

> "When she's not asleep, she's crying; as soon as I look away from her, she starts whining. In the morning, sometimes, she sleeps well, but as soon as she wakes up, off she goes again. She doesn't seem to be able to be alone much. I'm just rushing around all day long. She always cries at the wrong moment! So I take her out for walks to try to settle her down, and I set myself a goal for each walk we do. Even with the older one, when we used to go for a walk, there was always a purpose to it. They say when you have two kids, there's more love, but for me, well, it's as if I've been cut it in half. The big one used to cry when she came home from nursery, too. It's like a whirlwind, there's always one of them crying!"

I commented that it seemed to me that what was important was that there should not be any crying! And because Fanny did not cry when she was carried, or put to the breast, I asked the mother if she enjoyed breast-feeding her. At that point, she burst into floods of tears. Eventually she told me that she had used to enjoy feeding the elder daughter. But with Fanny, she had always felt stressed. She explained to me that Fanny was born a week early. She had therefore been unable to rest or to prepare herself for the birth. And when she had to go to hospital, she was not ready. Right now she felt completely de-skilled with her baby. Also, she felt a huge time pressure, both on a daily basis and in terms of her maternity leave. She concluded by saying that it had all started on All Saints' Day, when she had found herself alone with the two children. I now had enough elements to construct a hypothesis of a failure of the first moment of the oral stage. The signifier that struck me was '*profiter*'. This, of course, put me on the track of pleasure and unpleasure, and so I asked her about how it went when she breast-fed Fanny.

She told me, as if to justify herself, that because the older one was there, she sometimes had to feed Fanny while she was giving the other one her bath or her tea, just like all mothers of two children have to. But even when she was alone with Fanny, she would sometimes read, or make a list of things to do, or things she had not yet managed to do during the day. This mother thus confirmed to me that what was at stake between her and her daughter was an absence of reciprocal pleasure.

I told her that I had imagined a scene while I was listening to her, and what I could see was little Fanny sleeping, but as soon as she moved, her mother would find herself saying inwardly, "She's going to wake up, and there's nothing for me to do but try to get her to stop crying." So Fanny would wriggle even more and start crying, doing precisely what her mother feared most. The mother said, "That's exactly it!" So, even when Fanny was sleeping and not crying, it was impossible for the baby or the mother to be in a state of pleasure. By now I was almost certain that we were dealing with a failure of the first time of the drive.

To make sure, I asked the mother if the two of them looked at each other during feeding. The mother sobbed as she told me that Fanny would always turn her head away, and so they could not see each other.

In other words, what had not taken place was the first time of the oral drive, when the baby feeds on the mother as much as the breast, but there is also the installation of a reciprocal look, which signals the first knotting of the 'scopic' drive.

I then asked her if she talked to Fanny. "Yes," she replied, "but only in my head."

This confirmed the lack of the installation of the register of invocation. The first stage of the register of the 'invocatory' drive is indeed the formidable appetite of the baby for the parent's voice.

How could Fanny possibly be satisfied with nourishment that was never seasoned with or made more tasty by the mother's presence? What could she cling on to if no look was directed at her, no words were addressed to her? The only modality of presence left to her was tears, her cries being the sole effect of the encounter and of support for her.

The fact that I had picked up on the way the mother spoke of the absence of pleasure was to have its effects. In the following session, I found the two of them sitting in the waiting room. I should point out that this time Fanny was awake, and the mother blurted out that she had told the child in advance that she must not go to sleep because they were coming to see me.

This was the first time I addressed the baby myself, and I said to her, while looking at her mother as well, that "Mummy talks to her a lot now." "It's like day and night," the mother said to me:

> "I realised I hadn't been taking the time to get to know her, so now my relationship with her has changed completely. It's as if she and I have 'fallen in love'! You told me to take time to enjoy being with her, and that's what I've done. And because she was always OK when she was on the changing mat, I've put more into those times. That little girl loves being massaged!"

Spontaneously, this mother was now able to make associations regarding the absence of pleasure between herself and her own mother. And when I pointed out to her that it had all started around All Saints' Day, which follows on from All Souls Day, she was finally able to talk about the very recent death of her mother, who had become an alcoholic.

I saw them twice more, and I left it to the mother to decide when the last session would be. She came back to see me three months later. By then, she had become one of those mothers who positively radiates maternal pride, and was thrilled to discover all the things her daughter could do. During this session, Fanny was sitting on her lap, and I noticed she was staring at a sphygmomanometer which was on the desk in my consulting room. I was a little concerned, because my knowledge as a 'shrink' had taught me that such a fixed stare at a particular object could often be a sign of depression in a baby. But, as her mother would soon show me, I was quite wrong. She pointed out to me that Fanny was fascinated by her own image, reflected alongside her mother's in the little mirror of the sphygmomanometer. So in fact, I was witnessing 'live' the enactment of the second time of the scopic drive, which is also called 'the mirror stage'. I fed back to her the excellent capacity she had developed to observe her daughter, and she was now able to say to me: "You know, my elder daughter is like her father in every way, but Fanny is so like me, and I'm just like my own mother." In other words, looking at Fanny was like looking at her own mother who had become an alcoholic and had now passed away.

Fanny's mother was able to make this enunciation during the last session we had, but it was possible above all because she had now been able to look differently at her daughter. It could have taken her several months otherwise, without the sessions, at that point in time when a baby simply cannot wait, and the relationship would have been severely damaged.

Clearly I could have placed the emphasis on the mother, and paid more attention to her own suffering. She had given me plenty of clues: the particular way she used the past tense when she spoke, her fusional nostalgia with her elder daughter, her difficulties in adjusting to managing with "two of them", her internal crying; all this indicated a depressive state.

But to focus on the mother's discourse and her affects would have meant passing over what was having an effect on her in the real, namely the encounter with her second baby. So it was around this encounter that the work had to be done, by looking at things from the baby's point of view.

What underpinned the direction of the treatment and gave the dynamic impulse which led to the reinstatement of the link between the mother and her baby, was that I allowed the baby to orientate us in finding the contingencies of this initial time of the drive.

Using this first time meant being alert to the absence of the disjunction of satisfaction in the baby, in other words, whatever it is that turns feeding into nourishment through the operation of a primary form of jouissance. It is precisely this knotting with a 'surplus of pleasure' which had not taken place, and which constituted a primary failure. Because at the same time, what had not been swallowed was also the absence of a primary incorporation of whatever would have had an effect of presence for Fanny. This explains why, even though she opened her mouth and took the breast, Fanny continued crying because she was never satisfied.

When the curtain of the lips closes, the scenario playing itself out in the mouth circles around a void. Today, Jeanne is a woman who through her own analysis had been taken right back to the baby she was herself.

Photos of her as a very small child show her opening her mouth as she bursts out laughing. Her mother would say to her, "As a baby, you were a little ray of sunshine," but she would add, "except when I was feeding you." Sitting in her mother's lap, Jeanne, who was by no means beautiful, would smile with her mouth wide open, as if it took up the whole of her face; even her eyes were laughing. But when her mother bent over to breast-feed her, the little baby's body stiffened, everything in her tensed up, she turned her head away, closed her mouth and pursed her lips. If her mother tried to force her to feed, she would howl and weep copiously. Her mother would become exhausted; sometimes, at her wits' end and unable to bear any more anxiety, she would lose her temper, and Jeanne would squirm around in her cot. In this particular battle, the baby was the winner. When she was two weeks old, she was hospitalised for more than three weeks, during which she did not see her mother. The medical staff had decided to take the feeding problem very seriously, treating it as a serious case of anorexia. The mother was left out of the picture, without any explanation, and with a sense of guilt which made her feel completely incompetent. Jeanne was tube fed. She put on weight and was sent home. And now the battle continued, though it was a less bitter one because Jeanne had learnt to resign herself to any situation. And because she could no longer express anything with her mouth by opening and closing her lips, she found another way of communicating which, alas, was far more painful. In order to put into circulation what it was that had failed during this first moment of the oral stage, the entire rim and the contour of her mouth became covered with purulent impetigo. Opening her mouth became a form of torture, making her sob with pain, and at those times nothing in the world could satisfy her. Once again she was hospitalised, and this time for even longer. Later on, the chronic impetigo faded, and the symptom became localised lower down, around the pharynx, which meant she now suffered from pharyngitis and tracheitis, as a result of which she was often sent to stay with her paternal grandmother, which involved further and repeated separations from her mother. The only gains in all this were that Jeanne's mother now felt less guilty, and Jeanne herself was distanced from her mother, spending long periods with her grandmother. While she was with her grandmother, she was not only the most beautiful baby in the world, but was also shielded from her mother's projections.

On the other hand, what was really at stake remained completely unnoticed.

Taking a broader look at the moments of tension around feeding would have offered some enlightenment. The mother would scarcely look at the baby's face, which lacked any attractive features; all her attention was centred on the little skull covered in cradle cap. The mother, while breast-feeding, would be busy scratching off the scabs. Her frenzied activity certainly had a function, as we discovered later, masking her anxiety and depression. The work of analysis, indeed, allowed us to construct a case in which Jeanne as a baby had become her mother's depressing object. There might seem to be very little difference between Jeanne's situation and that of Fanny, who was also caught up in her mother's depression, but the difference was that Jeanne had chosen to be active by resolutely closing her mouth. She showed through her crying, and with great determination, that she simply had to refuse what was offered.

It is vital that we take into account the strength with which a baby can say no and refuse what is offered. It is often a primordial refusal, indicative of a psychical position which we need to be alert to.

According to G. Cullere-Crespin, "a refusal at the level of feeding may be a translation, from the baby's point of view, of an attempt to place a limit on maternal intrusion, which sometimes takes place at another level".[7] Jeanne, by refusing both the breast and the bottle, to the point of going hungry, was saying no to her mother and to the depression, of which she had become the object. By not engaging with the first time of orality, or by entering into it in the mode of negation, she not only showed that she was not receiving the little extra we discussed earlier, but also that she was energetically refusing the place assigned to her in her mother's psychical economy. This tiny baby also demonstrated her own psychical good health and an astonishing capacity for analysis. It was a pity that the medical staff did not learn the lesson she was offering them. This growing baby ended up opening her mouth and feeding normally, once she discovered the power of words. She certainly used them more than others and especially with her mother, whose feelings she could no longer spare. Once she became an adult and could be awakened by analysis, she chose yet again to use her mouth, becoming a professional in a field involving the art of speech. So in the outcome of this analytic treatment, perhaps we can discern a singular way of regaining the little extra that was missing from the first time of the oral stage, and weaving it into her life.

Second time: 'sucking oneself'

During the second, reflexive, time we know that babies find an object of satisfaction on their own body. This is based on the assumption that something has operated successfully at the first time, and this means we need to return to what is at stake in that process for an ordinary baby. We know that during the first time, the baby is attached to an 'extra pleasure' which summons the other. Lacan pointed out that the baby certainly takes part in this, by playing at letting go of the nipple or the teat, then latching on again, then letting go again. In this game of latching on and letting go, Lacan observed "something active enough for us to be able to be able to articulate it in the sense of a desire for weaning".[8] From this point of view, Lacan affirmed once again that "it's not true that the child is weaned. He weans *himself*".[9]

But this first weaning, this initial movement of separation, can take place only against a background of presence. It is only if a baby has succeeded in weaving around the breast/bottle an extra pleasure at the level of the other, and has not merely sucked on a bit of mucous membrane and swallowed some milk, that it is possible to let go in the secure knowledge that it can be re-found. Fundamentally, one never weans oneself from nothing but from something. How else could we conceive of "the very primitive facts, which are quite primordial in their appearance, of the refusal of the breast, the first forms of anorexia whose correlations at the level of the Other our experience teaches us to seek out right away?".[10] And it is precisely this little something of the Other that babies seek to re-find for themselves on their own body.

What is operating at the second time, then, is a primary displacement and a primary symbolic inscription. And the operator being activated belongs to the register of separation, of the cut.

So what happens when this operation does not take place?

Failure of the second time

I am going to examine a case of anorexia in a baby, in the light of a failure of this second time. An interruption of the clinical work right in the middle of the sessions will, I hope, show how the theory of the drives can shed light on the paradoxes inherent in the clinic of orality, and open up new pathways for intervention.

Let us look at how Rosalie entered into the circuit of the oral drive, and how she fared in it. She was ten months old when she was brought to see me because she was refusing to feed following weaning, which had taken place at her mother's instigation.

Right at the start, the mother said to me,

"All she wants is the breast. And I just couldn't do it any more. I felt I had to be there for her all the time, spend all my time with her. It always had to be just the two of us. I could never feed her if I wasn't alone with her, she insisted that I should isolate myself. And it was impossible to do anything else at all."

While the mother was talking, I watched as Rosalie snuggled up against her. She was sitting on her lap, with her head literally stuck to the breast, or else she would try to clamber up her mother's body so she could take even firmer possession of it, or at least reassure herself it would not slip away from her.

As we know, at the first time of the circuit, the baby grabs on to the object of satisfaction, in Rosalie's case, the breast. And in order for the first time to be operative, something else has to come into play and weave itself into the circuit alongside the milk, so that the baby does not feel it is merely reduced to an alimentary canal that will be filled with warm liquid. This other something, as we have seen, is the warmth, the smell, the voice, the heartbeat of the maternal other. Put another way, in this operation, it is necessary that the mother makes a gift of something of herself, as well as of the breast or bottle. It is with this that something of a presence can become inscribed, and that the baby can experience not only organic repletion but also symbolic repletion. This knotting of nourishment and feeding which operates at the first time will have an effect of presence, and allow the process of separation-individuation, which is played out at the second time, to take place.

In Rosalie's case, we can assume that there had been some failures in the knotting process. At first sight, there was a sense that the mother felt saturated and overwhelmed, and this perhaps did not allow her to give away anything of herself, to give her daughter a surplus of herself, this precious little extra. It seemed that Rosalie had been suspended at this second time after she was weaned. Since then, she had stopped eating all together, and her mother told me that she did not even put anything into her mouth. Now, she said, she was obliged to force-feed her. Sobbing copiously, she explained how she would put her in the high chair, push back her head, and shove in the spoonful of food. And Rosalie acquiesced to this! It was this passivity that intrigued me. The only way I could make sense of her allowing herself to be force-fed was to read it as a lack of differentiation between "hand and mouth".

Everything seemed to indicate that Rosalie could not stop swallowing her mother, as if she had to remain perpetually linked to her, and could not bear any cut or separation. And indeed it was a problematic of separation, to be precise, of an impossible separation; when Rosalie wanted something, she did not move, but grabbed hold of her mother's hand, expecting her to take hold of the object in order to satisfy her. It seemed that the mother's hand extended into Rosalie's mouth, and vice versa. The mother also told me that Rosalie did absolutely nothing physically.

It was in the course of working very precisely with this point at the second time of the circuit of the drive, where separation becomes operational, that something could be altered and shifted in Rosalie's case.

I suggested seeing them together with the father, and I placed an emphasis on motricity, inviting them to assume that Rosalie was capable of getting herself moving.

But I had it all wrong! In the next session, the endless feeding which had been playing out on the side of the mother was displaced onto endless walking up and down as Rosalie was held by her father. He was very proud to show me how his daughter would grab onto his hands and could not stop walking up and down as she clung on to him. The two of them together could have just walked like that for the whole session. And yet, Rosalie did not look in the least pleased. In other words, there was no trace of jouissance. I decided to introduce a cut myself. Since she was sitting beside the toy box, I suggested she could take a toy for herself. She looked to see what there was and then, without moving, looked meaningfully at her mother. I asked her again, encouraging her to stretch out her arm. But she remained firmly in position. She made disapproving sounds, looked at her mother again, straight in the eye, and carried on making grumbling noises. Seeing that nothing was coming to her, Rosalie became furious, threw herself on the floor, and lying on her stomach, howled and beat the floor with her fists. She remained in a state of anger, so I suggested to the mother that she could pick her up.

A moment later, as she was still crying, I held out the box of tissues to her. Without a shadow of hesitation, she grabbed her mother's hand, issuing a very clear order that she should take a tissue for her. I intervened quite firmly, saying to her that if she could take Mummy's hand then she could also take a tissue herself. She determinedly refused, and began crying more loudly. I noticed that she was still staring at the box of tissues, so I offered them to her again. This time, after a short pause, I watched as she held out her arm and took hold of the tissue. I congratulated her, encouraged her, and I was surprised to see Rosalie settle down a bit further away, separate from her mother, which she had never done before. I then watched as she took advantage of our conversation to go and rifle through her mother's handbag. She pulled out a little pack of tissues, and against all expectations put it greedily into her mouth.

The mother could not get over it, we were witnessing a moment of real pleasure. Pleasure and amazement, just as when babies enjoy seeing themselves mirrored in their mother's eyes. This is also how they move on into the third time of the drive. All at once, I realised that after this experience of pleasure, during which she herself had put the pack of tissues into her mouth, Rosalie would stop refusing to feed.

Something of the nature of a cut had had an effect in this case. It allowed Rosalie to engage in the process of separation, and at the same time in the second time of the circuit of the drive, which is the stage of autoerotism. To better understand how necessary this operation is, we need to return to the question of what it was that had 'failed' at the first stage.

The mother had told us that Rosalie never stopped demanding the breast, as if she was never full. This demand was like the Danaides' barrel. There was 'no end' to it, wearing out the desire of the mother, although the latter never failed to be present. What did the child make of this?

Their reciprocal exhaustion and absence of pleasure were obvious. And yet we cannot doubt that the breast had been put in the place of an erotic object, and the mother seemed to have offered it with all the trappings usual for the primal seducer, as Freud had described in the *Outline*.[11] Could we then think in terms of this mother being unable to give up something of herself, to make a gift of herself? This was by no means apparent, given the way in which she would offer herself to the child to be devoured; it was more a case of her giving herself without any restraint or limits.

So what does an ordinary mother do at the first time in order for the baby to be taken up in the circuit of the drive and the dynamic of desire? Firstly, she does not always respond strictly at the level of needs, in terms of instant saturation. She is capable of imagining that her baby has desires for something other than that. We can observe this when a mother feeds words to her baby who is howling with hunger. The mother speaks to her baby while preparing for the feed, and you can see the child clinging on not so much to the nipple as to the sounds of 'motherese'. Then, like an echo, the baby will respond by babbling, which will have the power to melt the mother's heart. So there is something like a 'non-response', a primordial refusal which has a place alongside primary satisfaction, and which rests on the supposition of a subject in the baby.[12] This is what allows for the inscription of the symbolic and for access to a desire which is mediated by the Other.

Fundamentally, alongside the gift of the mother, there needs to be a 'barring' of the mother – and this is something to which less attention is paid. Yes, there needs to be a gift, but not too much!

It was certainly this lack which was lacking for Rosalie when I first met her. And it was the presence of a lack which I brought into being by activating the process of separation. Because the satisfaction of the drive in the oral register is not actually eating but rather a pleasure obtained through the mouth. It is words that make our mouth water when we look at a restaurant menu; we can enjoy food without eating it. And this was exactly what Rosalie had not previously tasted.

Third time: making oneself sucked

The third Freudian time is the crucial one, because is that point what is at stake is the possibility of a vicissitude of the drive that will play a radical part in the course of psychical development. It is a time that marks a turning point, because, as we have seen, it follows from a reversal into its opposite. Where the oral drive is concerned, it is the moment when the activity of sucking is reversed into passivity: being sucked. Let us recap: in this turning around, Freud noted a double movement: not only that from activity to passivity but also a reversal with regard to content. The babies who up to this point have actively sought to connect with the object of satisfaction, and then to find it on their own body, will now turn away from this self-satisfaction, and make themselves into the object of satisfaction for the other. It is precisely here that we find a reversal, from tending towards the object into making oneself into an object, so that the babies find themselves in a completely different position. In this operation, in which infants lend themselves to the satisfaction of the other, we can say that they are both the object and the subject of this satisfaction. By lending themselves to it actively, there is the production of a new subject, and that is the crucial aspect of the third time.

Lacan's discovery was to make this time that of "making oneself done to[13]". But why did Lacan not remain satisfied with the Freudian notion of passivity? What is the function of this new twist towards passivisation? Because, as a reader and interpreter of Freud, his rigour led him to focus on the aspect of what is actually operative. Freud had told us that the third time produces "a new subject" to which one shows oneself in order to be looked at.[14] The third time thus constitutes an unavoidable moment in the establishment of a position resolutely turned towards the other. It is even the condition for the mark of the Other to be able to make an inscription.

Whereas in the first time babies move towards the object of pleasure and satisfaction, at the third time they seek to provoke pleasure in the other by making themselves the object of satisfaction. *We can thus be sure that with this third time, the baby becomes a subject at the same time as producing one.*

The operative factor in this important moment of structuring, and that which produces something of the subject, therefore also opens up the field of narcissism. Let us unpack this question a little: when babies seek to provoke pleasure in the other, when they go to any lengths to delight the other they make themselves the object of satisfaction for the other and thus produce a new subject; but they themselves are also undeniably subjects of this pleasure, which they are so good at provoking. Marie-Christine Laznik noted a very fine illustration of this moment in an advertisement for Pampers.[15] A baby is lying completely naked on a changing mat. While changing her baby, the mother plays at nibbling the baby's foot. Goodness, you could simply eat this baby up! Because he is playing too, and what he is doing is just that – getting his little feet eaten up. He holds out his little tootsies and his eyes are riveted by his mother's mouth pretending to eat them up. What this baby wants, what he provokes, is not just an orgy involving his toes, but also the laughter coming from his mother. At that moment, the baby's look shifts, it is no longer focussed on the mother's mouth, but rather on her eyes as she bursts out laughing. By doing this, he actively brings about a change in his mother. We might even say that he is the subject of another subject in her, since she changes from being the devouring mother to the laughing mother. Fundamentally, what occurs at this third time is the bringing into being of something of subjectivity, as much for the other as for himself. This is why the field of narcissism is involved in the second part of 'Drives and their Vicissitudes'.[16] *So the third time becomes a structural turning point where the field of narcissism is introduced in so far as it passes via the Other.*

Failure of the third time

We have seen that the passivisation involved in the third time has the effect of the inscription of narcissism in the link with the other. It is the advent of one subject for another subject that is knotted into place here. So any failures at the third time will have an effect on structure.

This is why Marie-Christine Laznik has made the third time into an operative landmark in diagnosis. Indeed, babies at risk of autism never pass through this time; so for them, there is no question of a reversal. They may move towards the object, but they will never take the risk of provoking pleasure in the other by making themselves the object of the other's jubilation.

Because of this, babies at risk of autism are not fully caught up in the circuit of the drives. They may throw us off the scent at both the first and the second times, but they will not have access to the inversion in which they actively make themselves the subject of pleasure in the other. All therapeutic work is thus aimed at enabling them to achieve this. Their access to the first time, if it is possible, is conditioned by a degree of desensitisation, because babies at risk of autism, far from lacking empathy, suffer from having too much of it. These babies are endowed with such sensitivity to the other that any encounter will disorganise them to a very high degree. We are grateful to Marie-Christine Laznik for having introduced us to the work of Adam Smith on the excess of empathy in these babies.[17] Autism, viewed from this angle, appears to be a pathology of excess and not of lack. Clinical work to enable these children to pass through the first time amounts to desensitising them, by approaching them only via a single channel of sensitivity, as I was able to do with little Victor.[18] As for the second time, this is always present in such babies since their lives are largely taken up with autoerotic movements. Except that if we observe them closely, we find it would be more correct to speak of automatic movements, since there is no erotic dimension, nor the libidinisation of the object on which autoerotism is based. It is precisely the aspect of eroticisation that needs to be introduced for these small subjects, because they suffer from never having been animated by it. This is why clinical work with these babies always consists in a psychical resuscitation.

Marianne, aged seven months, seemed to have become stuck in this absence of Eros with her mother.[19] She was not a particularly engaging baby, she did not initiate any movement, and if anyone picked her up, her hypertonia prevented her from cuddling. But above all, she quite obviously avoided her mother, who herself had contributed to this dynamic. Marianne's first few months of life were spent being moved from one place to another. Her mother had run away from the maternity ward, repeating what her own mother, in the throes of a psychotic breakdown, had inflicted on her as a baby. She finally returned to her foster family, and then met a man who put an end to the unstable situation by reporting to social services the ill-treatment Marianne was suffering.

That is how mother and baby arrived at the unit.[20] The withdrawn state of the baby and her avoidance of contact were blatant, and seemed to be aimed exclusively at the mother. Indeed, the latter never stopped acting intrusively towards her daughter, and would short-circuit any initiatives the baby would take. For a long time, this withdrawal was interpreted as a vital defence in the sense understood by Selma Fraiberg.[21]

But Marianne was not only putting her energy into avoiding her mother. The more we spoke about her in our 'baby meeting',[22] the more we felt we were in the presence of the extinction of her appetite for the Other. When she was ten months old, the team were still concerned about her slow development, the persistence of hypertonia and above all her lack of appetite for any kind of relationship. My colleagues would certainly describe a few interactions which seemed not to be entirely devoid of pleasure, but their very detailed descriptions did not persuade me that the third time of the circuit of the drive had been put into place, which constitutes a very early sign that there is a risk of autism. So it was not simply a case of agreeing to see her and of treating it as a case of defensive withdrawal. What was needed was to capture something of the subject in the code of the Other. In clinical work with small babies there are, indeed, some subjects who for one reason or another are not caught up in language, and "the problem one encounters is a problem of capture".[23] In such cases, the baby has to be brought back into the drive circuit of exchange. On the part of the analyst, this means 'libidinising', in other words, inspiring something sexual via the drives.

Because the third time had not taken place for Marianne, I suggested to the team that I should see her individually, in addition to the treatment plan already in place.[24] Taking on a baby without the mother goes against received wisdom and ideologies regarding bonding, and often provokes silence and even resistance in some team members. What finally convinced my colleagues, however, was that they could see that this baby was developing outside of any kind of sexuality.

One of the most important functions of a mother is to introduce her baby to sexuality and jouissance, thus allowing the drives to become inscribed over the course of the first few months of life.

In the *Outline*, Freud even spoke of the mother-baby pair as "the prototype of all later love relations".[25] A very Freudian thing indeed, this insistence on sexuality, which is at the heart of the primal couple! There is indeed a primal jouissance which is necessary for babies to construct themselves in the link to the Other, which does not stem from either a "beyond the pleasure principle" or a "surplus of jouissance". Lacan noted it himself when he made the mother the one who "teaches her little one to parade".[26] It suffices to observe an ordinary mother to see how she quite naturally teaches jouissance to her baby.[27]

When she feeds the baby, when she gives herself, she cannot stop herself from touching the child. Delicately, she caresses the tiny fingertips, her lips rest on the minute hands, on the forehead . . . In return, the baby eats her with a look. This is the inscription of the first time of the oral drive. Then she looks at the infant, she cannot stop herself from doing so, and she is not embarrassed to think that hers is decidedly the most beautiful baby in the world: her little prince or princess. The baby is mirrored in those eyes, and finds it delightful. So at the same time, the first stage of the scopic drive is put into place. But the ordinary mother does even more: she talks to her baby, serenades him or her, seduces the child with her siren's voice,[28] and this also works towards the first stage of the invocatory drive. And as if that were not enough already, just see how she gives herself to the child, devouring him or her with her eyes, covering the baby with words of love . . . She simply cannot resist: "I could just eat that little baby right up!" But she restrains herself because jouissance "begins with a tickle and ends with a blaze of petrol".[29] So she makes sure that the jouissance does not catch fire; this is where she is barred, "not too much jouissance", as Lacan reminds us.[30] And so she pretends to nibble the little hand, the cute little tootsie. The baby, utterly delighted, pretends, too, holding out the little foot, pushing out the tummy, and waits, tense with pleasure, waiting to see the mother laugh, trying to make her laugh; and then bursts out laughing too, allowing us to witness 'live' the third time of the oral drive, which signals the advent of the subject. This is how a mother initiates her baby into jouissance. She eroticises the relation, without going as far as igniting the petrol.

This is exactly what had not taken place between Marianne and her mother. We might say that her experience alternated between fires that had died out, leaving her rigid and motionless, and the return of flames that burned her. But above all, Marianne did not seek to provoke jouissance in the Other. So there was only one thread I could follow: eroticising the relation on three levels – oral, scopic and invocatory – in order to work towards an inscription of the sexual.[31]

From the very first session, Marianne would quickly show signs of saturation. Encountering the Other seemed to cause her to break down in the most extreme way. She would tense up, turn away, tremble convulsively, and tears would pour down her cheeks. In spite of everything, I decided to follow my desire and rather than seeking to comfort her, I presented her with the box of tissues. Contrary to all expectations, she became interested in this. There followed a game of exchanges in which Marianne took hold of a tissue, tore it into shreds, and made little balls from it. Then she put one of the little balls into her mouth and chewed on it with satisfaction. In my very finest voice, and with all the lyrical embellishments I was capable of, I commented on this swallowing of a little piece of something good and pleasurable with Madame Couvert. I treated the little ball of tissue as something delicious and I decided to offer her a real feast. I picked up the famous box of tissues, and transformed it for the occasion into a box of serviettes. I knotted one around my neck and took care to deck out Madame H, the paediatric nurse responsible for her, in the same fashion. Marianne soon joined in the game, offering her own neck, and I covered her too in this garment of paper tissue, this little of piece of nimbus she had already fed herself on. We partied, it was a real joy, a 'Belshazzar's feast', as our grandmothers used to say! The 'spoons' went from one mouth to another. Each mouthful was followed by an exclamation which led to a chorus of "oh's" and "ah's", which Marianne soon took up. At the end of the session, I picked up all the little balls of tissue as if they were sacred peas, but also in their capacity as hand-made works of art, and put them into a box to keep as precious objects.

These exchanges in the register of orality evoked a lively pleasure, as much for Marianne as for my colleague and myself. Nothing was faked, indeed it could not possibly have been. I truly enjoyed those mouthfuls, and gladly took in all the 'spoonfuls' Marianne had given me. It was a game of oral joyfulness, which was both intense and serious. And yet there was nothing that could allow us to assume that the circuit of the third time of the drive had been put in place.

Marianne certainly experienced some pleasure, and there is no doubt that it was a good time for her. On the other hand, she never attempted to provoke any pleasure in me. In order to activate the reversal that signals the inscription of the third stage, I would have to repeat these scenes with their flavour of oral eroticism over and over again in the sessions. It was the only pathway that would assure Marianne of the consistency of my desire, so that she would be able to incorporate it in order finally to make herself the subject of a jouissance in the Other.

In parallel, I needed to work towards eroticising the other circuits. First of all there was the scopic drive, in other words, the drive concerned with the look my own just as much as Marianne's directed at me or at any other object that attracted her attention. And at the same time I aimed to activate the invocatory drived during our vocal exchanges.

When Marianne looked at my face during a session, I would show my delight in being looked at by her and show how flattered I was to be the object of her attention. I heard myself saying, for example, "What a lucky person Madame Couvert is that you're looking at her so carefully and so intently. It's really lovely to be looked at like that!" I drew Madame H, the paediatric nurse, to one side, and said to her, "After all, Madame H, we don't often get the chance to be looked at so closely!" And I genuinely thought it; not being looked at by a baby is a truly unbearable experience. I thought to myself, recalling Ponti,[32] that she had the eyes of an explorer, and I said ecstatically, "Marianne with her explorer's eyes!" All of a sudden I noticed that I was also looking intently at her myself, and I described aloud and with pleasure all the things her little being offered for me to look at: her eyes, so present and lively but also still, mistrustful; her little mouth, which still hardly dared to say anything; and her ears, which seemed to listen very carefully. If Marianne's look alighted on my bracelet, I would make it come to life just for her. Any object that Marianne had designs upon would come alive as if by magic. So all the conditions seemed to be in place for the circuit of the scopic drive to take its course through the three stages. And yet each time the question of 'desire' came into it, things would become uncertain. Because Marianne kept looking at a little doll, half-fairy, half-princess, I deduced that she wanted it. I picked up the pretty little figurine and made her fly very gently towards Marianne. She held out her arms to grab hold of the doll she so longed for, but the moment she got hold of it, she seemed to become cross. Marianne let go of the doll, waving her hands as if to get rid of it. But her look was still fixed on it, and she very much wanted to grasp the object again. She tried to do so, and seized hold of the tiny little girl again, but once again was overcome by trembling. Again she became cross, and threw the doll down as if the whole of her upper body was convulsed by an electric shock.

This struck me forcefully, and a moment later I began to hesitate. Over the years of clinical experience, I had come to regard such bodily events as very valuable indicators. They are fertile moments at which something of the subject is in the process of being produced. At such moments, I make sure that I stay with what the baby has given me to understand, and strive for a rigorous reading of what is being communicated.

I had formed the hypothesis that over the course of the sessions, Marianne had been able to be an object of great desire in the transference, and that she had now been able to project this desire onto the little doll, with which she was now identified. The problem was that for Marianne, desire had always been something that burned too fiercely; by touching it, she was exposing herself once again to being put into the place of that object which, once it was picked up, would be tossed around, handled roughly, or even maltreated, before being rejected.

So I picked up the little doll with the greatest possible care, and stroked it gently, saying that she certainly had good reason to mistrust me, but that grown-ups were supposed to take care of babies, and that where we were now, babies were taken care of. With hindsight, I would certainly have acted differently. In the light of *Seminar VI*, which opens up a field of interpretation which cannot be re-absorbed into the operation of the signifier, I would certainly have been able to stay closer to what Marianne was showing me.[33] I would have conveyed that whatever it was that she wanted, her body could not bear. Nonetheless, something did become operative, and Marianne was able to pick up the doll again, bringing it slowly right up to her face, and allowing herself to be stroked by the doll's hair, with its soft woolly strands. It seemed that she could now give herself something good, and could remain in a state of pleasure. This is exactly what signals the second time of the circuit, the reflexive and autoerotic stage.

However, the scene that followed showed us that Eros was quite absent from these exchanges, and that there was still no element of jouissance provoked by and taken from the Other. Marie-Christine Laznik has also commented that without Eros, autoerotism shrivels up and produces autism.[34] In other words, there was nothing yet to allow us to think that Marianne had arrived at a place where pleasure could be provoked and shared, which would have signalled that the third stage of the circuit had been completed. It would take time and considerable tenacity in order for this to occur. Over time, Marianne showed more and more appetite for the sessions, and each time would show great pleasure when she saw the miniature doll, which was in some way her double. There was one session which seemed to me to be crucial: she tried to carry the doll on her back. I congratulated her for being so brave, and encouraged her. She looked at herself in the mirror, contemplating herself with the doll sitting on her shoulders. I complimented her again, and praised her while speaking as if I were her: "Me, I'm looking after the little princess-doll, I'm taking care of her, I'm looking at her, I'm carrying her, I'm coaxing her . . ."; and then I added, "Madame Couvert is looking after Princess Marianne."

She seemed delighted with this subjectivising operation. She literally drank in my words, and I thought to myself that we were working with jouissance linked to the inscription of the invocatory drive because, echoing my enthusiastic exclamations, Marianne started to babble at the same frequency. She seemed to be so satisfied that I thought I could even hear her 'bubbling' with joy. This was followed by a new game: in an unexpected outpouring, suddenly she was kissing the doll. She kissed its feet; then, without hesitating, I did the same: I gently kissed Princess Marianne's feet. She then kissed the doll's feet again, I kissed hers again, and then she held out her feet for even greater pleasure, and so it went on several times. I was very pleased, thinking that perhaps, finally, the third time of the circuit of the drive had been inscribed; and then Marianne confirmed that this was the case.

It was the end of the session, the moment for goodbyes, because it was also our last session. I was just about to squeeze her hand, as I have always done with babies. But Marianne decided otherwise, she leaned her head against my cheek, and I, unable to resist, returned her kiss. It was a first in my work with babies, a sacred moment . . . Marianne had managed to relieve me of a piece of 'know-how', and together we had turned it into a piece of bespoke know-how.

Two factors are crucial here. First of all, we need to be able to be sensitive to babies' very early responses and to the absence of traits which are signs of the inscription of the link to the Other, and for this we need tools to orientate ourselves. And then we need to review our practice, a practice which always encourages us to think anew and dare to be inventive, based on the singularity of the subject who is coming into being.

Before Marianne, I had never worked alone with a baby, and I had never dared to bring jouissance into the clinic to such an extent.

Notes

1 J. Lacan, '*Anxiety*', op. cit. p. 231.
2 J. Lacan, '*The Four Fundamental Concepts*', op. cit. p. 166.
3 J. Lacan, 'Anxiety', op. cit. p. 232.
4 Ibid. p. 231.
5 D. Meltzer and M. Harris Williams, 'The Place of Aesthetic Conflict in the Developmental Process', in *The Apprehension of Beauty*, Perthshire, Clunie Press, 1988, pp. 7–39.
6 G. Cullere-Crespin, *L'épopée symbolique du nouveau-né*, op. cit. 2007, p. 62.
7 G. Cullere-Crespin, *L'épopée symbolique du nouveau-né*, op. cit. p. 62.
8 J. Lacan, '*Anxiety*', op. cit. p. 327.
9 Ibid.
10 Ibid.
11 S. Freud, *An Outline*, op. cit. p. 188.
12 Here I am taking up again something I wrote about in detail in: "La place de l'objet vocal dans la construction du lien", in M. Dugnat, ed., *L'art d'accommoder embryons, foetus et bébés*, Toulouse, érès, 2014, p. 149.
13 G. Cullere-Crespin, '*L'épopée symbolique du nouveau-né*, op. cit. p. 59.
14 S. Freud, 'Drives', op. cit. p. 129.
15 M.-C. Laznik, 'Des psychanalystes qui travaillent en santé publique', op. cit. p. 103.
16 S. Freud, 'Drives', op. cit. p. 134.
17 A. Smith, "The empathy imbalance hypothesis of autism: A theoretical approach to cognitive and emotional empathy in autistic development", *The Psychological Record*, 59, 2009, pp. 273–94.
18 See below the sections on 'The invocatory drive' and 'Failure of the first time'.
19 Here I am taking up a case which can be found in 'Des bébés exposés à la maltraitance et à la carence. À propos d'un dispositive particulier de cure', in H. Bentata, C. Ferron and M.-C. Laznik, eds, *Le bébé dans tous ses états*, Toulouse, érès, 2018.
20 The unit referred to here is the Clairs Vallons parent and baby unit of the paediatric medical centre in Ottignies, Belgium. This unit for joint hospitalisation takes in children and their parents, usually for a full-time long-term stay. The objectives of the work aim at the construction and consolidation of the bond between parent and baby. The family groups of two or three receive intensive and multidisciplinary treatment.

21 S. Fraiberg, 'Pathological Defences in Infancy', *Psychoanalytic Quarterly*, 51, 1981, pp. 612–35.

22 This is a weekly meeting centred exclusively on one baby residing in the unit. This was established because the severe problems of the mothers tended to take up all space for thinking, leaving the babies out of the equation.

23 J.-A. Miller, 'Interpréter l'enfant', in *Le savoir de l'enfant*, Paris, Navarin, 2013, p. 25.

24 In the unit, all the babies benefit from care which involves relational closeness: sessions of psychomotricity, and sessions in the therapeutic crèche twice a day.

25 S. Freud, *An Outline*, op. cit. p. 188.

26 J. Lacan, *'The Other Side of Psychoanalysis'*, op. cit. p. 78.

27 In her paper *'Godente ma non troppo* – le minimum de jouissance de l'Autre nécessaire à la consititution du sujet', in *L'enfant entre désir et jouissance*, Paris, Cahiers de l'Association lacanienne internationale, 2006, pp. 13–27, Marie-Christine Laznik very clearly delineated this maternal function of the initiation into jouissance, based on a rereading of Lacan's Seminars XVII and XVIII.

28 H. Bentata, 'Sirène et Chofar. Incarnation mythique et rituelle de la voix', in F. Meyer, ed., *Quand la voix prend corps. Entre la scène et le divan.* Paris, L'Harmattan, 2000.

29 J. Lacan, *'The Other Side of Psychoanalysis'*, op. cit. p. 72.

30 J. Lacan, *'Le Seminaire Livre 18, D'un discours qui ne serait pas du semblant'* (1970–1), ed. J.-A. Miller, Paris, Seuil, 2006, p. 108.

31 At the time, I had not realised the importance of the dimension of the tactile in the field of the drives; as we shall see, however, it is by no means absent.

32 C. Ponti, *L'arbre sans fin*, Paris, École des loisirs, 2007.

33 J. Lacan, *'The Seminar Book 6, Desire and its Interpretation'* (1958–9), ed. J.-A. Miller, Cambridge, Polity, 2019.

34 M.-C. Laznik, 'Des psychanalystes qui travaillent en santé publique', op. cit., p. 104.

Chapter 4

The field of specularity

Marie Couvert

Specularity is the second field of the drive discussed by Freud and taken up by Lacan. Freud chose to give it prominence because he observed that the operation of the look takes place in a sphere well beyond that of need. On the basis of the polarity voyeurism-exhibitionism, he attempted to grasp what it is that 'drives' the look, and manifests itself through irrepressible movements of visual tracking and offering something to be looked at. Such movements are involved in the looks exchanged between ordinary babies and their primordial other. The capacity of newborns to look their mother straight in the eye stems from an extremely early form of voyeurism, and their talent for getting themselves looked at is unrivalled. In this register, what is involved is not the capacity to see as it relates to the infant's sensorial apparatus, but rather the action of looking with its dimension of fascination. From this point of view, babies born blind are capable of seeing very well. Indeed, an experiment was carried out by Colwyn Travarthen on this subject: he filmed a mother singing to her baby who had been born with no vision at all. We see the blind baby's eyes fixed on his mother's look, while he beats time with his little hand.

When Lacan took up the question of the function of the look, he elaborated it further and it would become a central pivot in the psychical development of newborn babies. This is because the baby looking deep into the mother's eyes discovers a first mirror, and at the same time "the radical function of mirage which is included in the eye's first functioning". Fundamentally, "The fact that the eye is a mirror already implies its structure in some way."[1] At that moment, human babies grasp the dimension of the imaginary, and this knotting will have structuring effects for them. Lacan's *tour de force* was to show how failures in the scopic field can determine the child's psychical destiny in one way or another. Thus, the look constitutes an essential diagnostic feature, and is an especially valuable tool in differentiating the field of autism from that of the psychoses. It is also a lever that can be operated in the direction of the treatment of newborn babies.

First time: looking at oneself

As is the case with all the drive circuits, the scopic drive follows a trajectory consisting of three times. During the first time, known as the active stage, babies turn toward the object of satisfaction. During the second time, which is reflexive or autoerotic, they take themselves as the object of satisfaction. During the third, passive, time they make themselves the object of satisfaction for the other. This is the stage of "making oneself seen".[2] It is thus a stage of psychical structuration, during the course of which something of the subject comes into being; but it is also possible that the latter will not occur.

Looking, looking at oneself, making oneself looked at – these are the elements in the montage of the circuit of the scopic drive. Except that, if we read Freud carefully, we notice that he gives a very specific detail which is often overlooked. Whereas logical time imposes the primacy of activity over reflexivity, he insists that where the scopic drive is concerned, the opposite is true: "For the beginning of its activity the scopophilic drive is autoerotic."[3] It is only later that it can turn towards something else. In any case, let us recall something that Lacan pointed out: autoerotism does not mean indifference to the other.

> Newborns are far from being uninterested in whatever comes into their field of perception. There can be no doubt that there are objects deriving from the earliest period of the neo-natal phase. *Autoerotisch* can in no way mean a lack of interest in them.[4]

The only way we can understand and take account of this inaugural autoerotic stage, which partially determines how the circuits of the other stages will be established, is to remember that during this first time, since they are not indifferent to the other, babies seek to "see *themselves*" in the mother's eyes.

However, there is plenty of clinical evidence of babies who can see perfectly well but do not actually look. Why is that?

This is where the first stage is enlightening, and the fact that Freud explained that it is also autoerotic will take on its full value. What he grasped, and what is important, is that babies not only encounter an eye that sees them, but also a look which glorifies them. No baby would ever look the mother in the eyes if all there was to see was a mere reflection in a plane mirror. In order to enable us to understand this, Lacan takes up an experiment in optics, Henri Bouasse's "experiment of the inverted bouquet".[5]

The experiment is as follows: The observer is presented with an empty vase set up on a box which conceals a bouquet of flowers. Then, thanks to the presence of a concave mirror, the observer will see the vase with the bouquet in it. This optical illusion, which is a montage of a real object (the vase) and an image (the bouquet of flowers) is made possible only because the observer looks from a certain point of diffraction of the rays emitted by the concave mirror.

Marie-Christine Laznik, who has a knack for reading Lacan, invites us to consider the following analogy: if the observer's eye is that of the mother, we

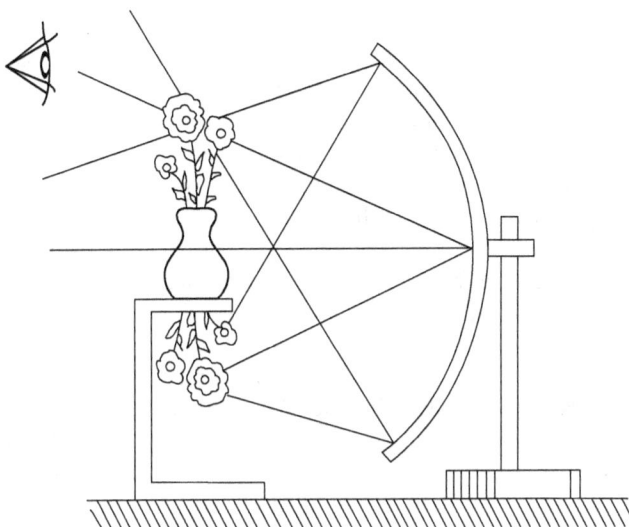

Figure 4.1

can deduce that the vase represents the baby's body, and the flowers the halo of glory, in other words, the fruit of the maternal other's unconscious desire for the baby.[6] The operation then consists in having a vision of a baby with a halo, in other words, decked out with the thousand attributes the mother will endow him or her with.

There are two things which allow the 'knotting' of the halo around the baby's head to take place: on the one hand, the axis of the mother's look, and on the other, the metaphor of the concave mirror. It is because the mother's look runs along the axis of illusion that she is capable of endowing the real child with every conceivable imaginary attribute. The child will then be able to identify with this image, which is the foundation of the image of the body and offers initial access to the imaginary register.

Failure of the first time

Bouasse's schema indicates that the mother, or whoever takes on the function of a primordial other, needs to be able to offer the baby the lure of a mirror which will produce the halo. Fundamentally, what the child invests can only be the investment that is offered to him or her. This is why the experiments conducted by Mary Ainsworth, such as the *Still face* or the *Strange situation* are so important, since they demonstrate the impact of an empty look from the mother, and its effects of withdrawal and flight in the baby.

On the other hand, what is less frequently mentioned is that newborn babies may make themselves looked at, or on the contrary may never initiate a look coming from an other. Some babies are more gifted at or better equipped to attract looks. In other words, failures do not take place only on the side of the other. The infant subject is also the more or less active agent of any look that alights on him or her. This is the case for babies at risk of autism, because their hypersensitivity means that the conditions for making eye-to-eye contact are less favourable; and this is also the case for babies who are suffering physically or are malformed. So there are particularities on the side of the baby which may have the effect of anaesthetising the parent's capacity for idealisation. Such babies are never considered as the most beautiful babies in the world, and if this short-circuit is not spotted, it may interfere with the establishment of the circuits of the drive.

This is what Theo taught me. Theo was a first baby, born by caesarean section following placental detachment. The mother described the birth as "a catastrophe". The anaesthetist and the gynaecologist argued over timings. Although she was under general anaesthesia, the mother was left with the memory of her body and flesh being cut into. The emergency doctor left her alone, and she had no spouse or partner to support her. When the baby came into the world, she was not able to hold him immediately. It was a boy, a big baby of more than 4 kilos. When he was finally placed in her arms, she noticed that his skull was a strange shape. She was told that he almost certainly had a premature suturing of the parietal bones. Soon it was confirmed that he had a craniosynostosis, which would limit the growth of his brain. She was, she told me, "just in floods of tears", and completely alone. They tried to reassure her by telling her that her baby was not in any pain; and he would soon be operated on. The "nerve doctor" confirmed that the baby's head was not painful, and that the operation would be completely painless.

As for Theo, he just howled and howled. He never stopped crying, day and night, until he had the operation. The mother told me she had spent four entire months doing nothing but try to soothe the baby. She had lost 12 kilos just watching him suffer. She could think of nothing else. She could see him caught up in his pain, she herself felt ill, and constantly reproached herself for having brought this suffering baby into the world. "He was in pain," she told me,

> "I think he had headaches. He was always red in the face, and nothing could calm him down. I picked him up, he was always lying on me, always on me, because no-one else could stand him, not even his father. I would hold him right up close to me for 40 minutes, crying all the time, till he finally went to sleep."

Then Theo had the operation, and she thought this could be the moment when things would start to change. And in fact, the way he cried did change. Now Theo no longer howled, but he would gently moan all the time; he just would not stop. That is why the mother came to see me, she had run out of ideas; she could see that her child was still suffering, whereas the doctors were trying to convince her that there was nothing wrong.

Throughout this time, as the mother spoke to me and told me all about Theo's first months, I watched the little baby sitting on her lap. I was disturbed to note that in the entire session, he would never look at me or at his mother. When she spoke to me, something seemed to upset him, he would wriggle, arching his back into a position of opisthotonus, and howling incessantly. It really seemed that this baby could not stand his mother doing anything other than hold him in this way, as if he needed this soothing envelope all the time. She added that there was nothing she could do when she breast-fed him. "He wants the whole of me," she told me, "and there I was dreaming of having a nice sociable baby who would enjoy being passed from one person to the next." And she so wanted him to take the bottle, to go to sleep in his cot . . . Her own mother told her off for picking him up all the time and turning him into an omnipotent baby. "And yet," she said, "I can't stop myself from picking him up, and I get so cross with myself when I expect too much of him!" At the same time, she was beginning to wonder; after all, Theo was now four months old, he was hardly a newborn any more.

Indeed, this mother had the remarkable intuition to realise not only that pain might completely overwhelm a baby, but also that it could leave traces behind.

The entire work of the *Project* was to show how babies already have at their disposal a ready-primed system to cope with the excitations that come at them from the external world. On the other hand, when faced with excitations coming from within, such as hunger and pain, newborns are completely defenceless. Babies need help from outside, in the form of intervention by those close to them, in order to be soothed. But what happens when a parent cannot offer this soothing envelope, because the baby's pain is not recognised or taken into account? Such babies cannot have experiences of satisfaction, or link moments of pleasure to an object. On the contrary, the repetition of pain breaks apart and prevents the process of linking. This will then constitute an inscription of trauma.

In fact, although Theo was no longer suffering, he could still remember suffering. This baby was still suffering from having been in such pain. It was the traces of suffering that still hurt. And this precious knowledge came to the mother, putting herself in the baby's place. She had been able to learn from him, while not bearing him a grudge for putting her into such a powerless position. I fed this back to her, because all this time she had been able to be there for her child, even if she had not been able to soothe him. She did not even bear him a grudge for not looking at her, because she had been so directly connected to her baby's pain. And moreover, the fact that this mother did not mention the absence of the baby's look did not mean she was incapable of noticing it. What determines things for the mother goes beyond the look, and involves the baby's own disposition to be able to orientate towards the other.

So the medical team had got it wrong; they would have done better to let themselves learn from the baby, instead of closing ranks behind their brand of knowledge in which this baby's suffering had no place.

Babies in pain are indeed unable to look, their pain threshold is constantly being exceeded, making them unavailable for any kind of relationship. This is why the absence of any look in a baby should always be of concern to the professionals.

There is good reason to explore the differential aetiology of this refusal to look, since it is present in babies at risk of autism as well as in those suffering from pain. Marie-Christine Laznik, indeed, deemed a failure at the first stage of the scopic drive to be a precursor of a diagnosis of risk of autism in the infant.[7] Things become more complicated if we agree that the baby at risk of autism may also suffer from not actually being able to engage in a look directed towards the other. And to this can be added a trajectory often strewn with neonatal complications; foetal suffering, painful labour, gastro-oesophageal reflux . . .

In order to avoid the risk of neglecting the scope of this 'non-look', perhaps we should speak in terms of the 'autistic syndrome', as Marie-Christine Laznik suggests.[8] In all cases, the absence of the baby's look causes a freezing of Bouasse's operation. And this is precisely what causes the failure. How could a mother, or any other primordial other, possibly engage in the illusion we have described in the presence of a newborn baby whose look slips away from you, avoids you, or is absolutely empty?

On the other hand, it is possible to marvel at a baby who has not stopped expressing the pain he or she is experiencing. One can marvel at the tenacity of a tiny child in never for a moment doubting in the mother, who is nonetheless worried. It seemed to me that Théo was one of those babies, gifted with a formidable strength, who had his own way of always 'looking' at his mother as the one who could come to his rescue.

This intervention was sufficient to enthrone Théo, elevating him to the rank of *His Majesty the Baby*. It was an absolutely fundamental operation of 'phallicisation', allowing the baby access to a primal imaginary, which could offer the foundation for his narcissistic inscription, that is to say, the pleasure ego (*Lust-Ich*) that Freud discussed.

We shall also see that this 'phallicisation' of the baby allows access to the setting in motion of the circuit that occurs at the second stage.

Second time: looking

The second time, which no longer operates exclusively through the mother's look, is the active stage, that of 'seeing', Lacan illustrated this moment of psychical structuring with the 'mirror stage'.[9]

It is also the only time that Lacan showed himself to be in any sense a developmentalist. Nowhere else in his teaching, which remained staunchly structuralist, did he approach the subject in such a psychogenetic way as in this stage, which he situates between the ages of 6 and 18 months. For Lacan, this was a pivotal moment in the process of development. The illustration he gave is of a completely ordinary experience, taken from the everyday lives of parent and baby. It is the moment when children turn towards the adult who is carrying them, and ask the parent to confirm, through their look or their spoken naming, that the one they can see in the mirror is indeed him- or herself. And the mother replies, "Yes, my darling, that's you!" In this way the mother, having been the glorifying mirror of the first stage, now has to facilitate the transition using something other than herself. She introduces into the heart of the dual relation with her child the function of a third term, represented here by the image reflected in the mirror, together with a nomination. Obviously the mirror is to be understood in a metaphorical sense, because as we shall see, what counts is not the actual physical mirroring but what is played out in it. Indeed, by introducing the Other, the mother frees her child from their capture in the imaginary. It is thus a fundamental experience in the construction of the child's ego, because it is precisely at this point that he or she enters into the field of the imaginary articulated with the symbolic. What the child now grasps in the mirror is no longer the glorified image as perceived in the mother's eyes; it is just a simple reflection. And the child is capable of identifying with this reflection, this image supported by the mother's assertion and recognised by everyone. From then on, everything takes place as if the little child can accept the materiality of the image as being the representative of his or her 'ego', and can knot it to the immateriality of an 'I'. We can observe here the double operation through which there is a knotting together of the dimension of the symbolic with a new kind of narcissism, new in the sense that it is now infused with the Other. "It is only when the child's relation to the mirror becomes doubly signifying that they can choose to establish a narcissistic relation with their reflection, and thus with their body."[10] The mirror now becomes a stage upon which children, by playing with their own reflection, can play with something of themselves while offering themselves to be looked at by the other. So the first stage of 'phallicisation', when we can see babies parading under the admiring gaze of their mother, is followed by that of the mirror stage, at which point the child enters into the game of the masquerade. The passage from parade to masquerade is decisive, because it demonstrates in an almost visible way that there has been a knotting together of the imaginary and the symbolic. Lacan invited us to grasp that masquerade "in the human domain" operates "not at the imaginary but at the symbolic level".[11] That is why this moment also constitutes a structural marker, because babies at risk of psychosis, while adept at parading themselves, will soon show themselves to be incapable of becoming involved in the masquerade.

Indeed, children who make the transition through the second stage now have access to a multiple reality shared with others, which protects them from psychosis; without this transition via the metaphor of the mirror, there is a risk that they will remain caught in the trap of a single code. To put it another way, the mirror is an obligatory pathway for the ordinary baby, to the extent that if it fails it leads to foreclosure. Foreclosure is a concept and a structural invention created by Lacan. We shall see that it constitutes a point of failure precisely where one would expect a knotting at the second time of the drive.

Failure of the second time

When the transition via the mirror stage does not take place, if it does not occur when it should, then it seems that the child's development will no longer be reversible. It is vital that we understand this essential point, which Lacan addressed with his concept of foreclosure. What is foreclosed is something that should happen by right but which does not occur in time. From a structural point of view, we need to delineate what exactly has not occurred within the given time frame. Clinical experience with premature babies can be enlightening here in relation to the scopic field, because it shows dramatically what it is that can fail at the second time of the inscription of the drive.[12]

Illan was a little boy aged 20 months, who had been admitted to our parent and baby unit.[13] He had been born very prematurely, and had a twin, another boy, who died aged three weeks in the neonatal unit; the mother had never managed to mourn the loss. Illan was very behind in his development; he had no language, and the way he encountered others was quite strange. He would jump up and down on the spot tirelessly, force his mouth into a smile, and wriggle the upper part of his body like a puppet; in a word, he was being a clown. One interpretation could have been that he put himself in the place of an antidepressant object for his mother, trying to cheer her up. However, during one session which I felt was crucial, Illan showed another kind of dificulty in our encounter. In the course of carrying out a test to evaluate his developmental age, I gave him some images to identify.[14] In concrete terms, it was a piece of wood with pictures of some objects familiar to a child: a bowl, a ball, a spoon . . . When I held out the piece of wood and asked him to show me the spoon, to my great surprise he tried several times to grab hold of it.

What failure was being manifested here? What had caused a child of 20 months to have no access to the symbolic? It is the montage of the circuit of the drives which will enlighten us. We shall see that it gives a valuable insight into Illan's case. For the time being, we need to take stock of the point in his trajectory at which this little boy's development was arrested.

At the moment when Illan wanted to grab hold of the spoon, as if the imaginary and the real occupied the same surface, I asked his mother about how he reacted in front of the mirror, which constitutes the second stage of the circuit. The mother told me that he never looked at himself. She had never seen him looking at himself in the mirror or playing in front of it. "He's just not interested," she said. I then asked her, focussing on the first stage, what she saw when she looked at Illan. Without hesitation, she replied, "His brother! I always see his dead brother when I look at him."

We can see clearly what had gone awry – the impossibility for this mother to look at her son without covering him with the mantle of his dead twin brother. How could Illan possibly have had the desire to look at himself in that first mirror, which consisted only in his mother's eyes full of grief?

What had failed for Illan shows that his mother had been unable to occupy the place of that first mirror, and could not send back a glorified image of himself to her baby. It is another way of saying that the 'phallicisation' of the baby stems from the mother's capacity for illusion.[15] But how could this mother create an illusion with an extremely premature baby and another baby who died so soon after he was born? This is precisely what is so difficult to establish between a mother and a premature baby.

Fundamentally, in cases of prematurity, it is the putting into place of the circuit of the drives that is compromised. There is no doubt that everything conspires to bring about a short-circuit at the first time of the drive. A baby who should not even be there yet, and is reduced to being the object of concern rather than admiration, is far from being *His Majesty the Baby*", but there is also the question of a mother without her baby and a baby without a mother[16] . . . So what happens when no other can come to occupy the place left vacant by the mother?

We can hypothesise that failures in the first time – in other words, vicissitudes linked to the putting into circulation of the drive – are bound to leave their imprint in one way or another on the destiny of the drive.

Let us come back to Illan, and see how the unpacking of the drive was also a valuable indicator for the direction of the treatment. We now knew why the first time of the drive had been subject to failures, and how Illan became captured by the reflection of his dead twin brother. Making this connection enabled the mother to speak of how fragile Illan had been at the time of the birth, while his twin brother was more robust. In her anguished imaginings, the mother had assumed that the one predestined to live was therefore the brother; for Illan, the outcome was far less certain. If we take these maternal unconscious representations to their logical conclusion, it was Illan who was already caught up in the web of death. This permutation, in the light of Bouasse's schema, had the effect of seating Illan firmly on a throne of death. It was only by working through the untangling of this superimposition that Illan could be liberated from the mantle of his dead brother, enabling him eventually to enter into the second time of the circuit of the drives.

Only on this condition would Illan be able to stop trying to grab hold of the drawing of the spoon, and would cease being a prisoner of the image. So we can see clearly how the impossibility of the putting into place of the mirror stage for the small child, that is to say the non-occurrence of the jubilation at the sight of his own image, could be the effect of a failure of the installation of the autoerotic look, which should have taken place at the first time of the drive.

But that is not all; the failure of the second stage also has an effect on the inscription of structure. The submerging of Illan in the image of his dead twin must surely have foreclosed the possibility of his capture in his own image. In other words, the failure of the second time of the scopic drive would also have compromised the conditions for an encounter with the reflected image, based on the distinction which operates between the imaginary and the real. The operation which takes place there is nothing other than the initial knotting with the Ego as an imaginary entity. Here we are at the crossroads of structure, where narcissism entwines itself with the drive, and we shall see that this is not without its consequences for psychical structure.

In 'Drives and their Vicissitudes', we saw that "Freud places narcissism at the heart of the process of the drives", while radically differentiating it from them, to the extent that, on close reading, it appears that there is something like a cut between them.[17] It is as if the paper were divided into two, "first, the deconstruction of the drive; secondly, the examination of *das Lieben*, the act of love".[18] Lacan explained it to us in his own way: "On one side, Freud puts the partial drives and on the other love. He says – *They're not the same.*"[19]

So I propose the following hypothesis: the field of narcissism, while it is distinct from the field of the drives, is closely intertwined with it. During the second time of the drive, at the pinnacle of the moment of jubilation when the baby suddenly perceives his or her own image, there must be a moment of see-sawing which is the basis of narcissism. As Safouan emphasises, there is a "structural twinning"[20] in which "the image of the mother and the image of the self become superimposed on one another in a double movement of identification and love".[21]

"The image of an elective object"[22] produced by the primordial other becomes fused with the drive jubilation linked to the assumption of one's own body in the image. On the one hand, there is identification, which emerges from the jouissance of the drive; and on the other hand there is the concurrent narcissistic inscription in the field of the Other. The two fields overlap and it is thus that "the self is loved because it is the beloved object of the Other".[23]

This is precisely what had failed for Illan; for him, 'I' was radically an other. We shall see that he was so totally alienated that he was also unable to gain access to the third time of the drive, which is that of the advent of the subject.

Third time: making oneself looked at

The third time of the circuit of the drive can only be set in motion provided that there is access to the dimension of the imaginary in so far as it is articulated with the symbolic. When, at the mirror stage, the mother says to her lovely little darling, "Yes, it's *you!*", the '*you*' is an invitation to the child to identify with all the possibilities that are not exhausted by the literal '*you*', exactly in the way that the word never fully overlaps with the thing. This is why the third time is that of the active manifestation of the subject.

At the third time, babies will actively try to attract the look of the other. They will do anything to get their mother to look adoringly at them. In doing this, they produce "the introduction of a new subject to whom one displays oneself in order to be looked at".[24] For this reason, Lacan made this passive third time one of intense activity. In other words, at the third time babies are seeking actively to make themselves the object of pleasure for the Other. Looking at this closely, we see that what appears at this last stage is of the order of a "signifying reversion".[25] Let us be clear: by making themselves the active agent of a pleasure provoked in the other, they are in a sense the subject of their own action, and at the same time they do not fail to produce a certain effect on the side of the other. This effect is what Freud called the appearance, for the baby, of "*ein neues Subjekt.*"[26] And Lacan pointed out that this subject which appears can also fail to appear: "not in the sense that there is already one, namely the subject of the drive, but in that what is new is the appearance of the subject".[27] This is a way of saying that there can always be failures, and that you cannot bank on this process in advance.

On the other hand, what is certain is that "it is only with its appearance at the level of the other that what there is of the function of the drive may be realized".[28] In order to grasp what is at stake at the third time of the drive in terms of a reversible function, we need to return to the paradigm of the drive chosen by Freud: voyeurism-exhibitionism. "What occurs in voyeurism? At the moment of the act of the voyeur, where is the subject, where is the object?" Lacan wondered.[29] And what he taught us is very valuable: in voyeurism, the subject is not situated at the level of the scopic drive, because, as he reminds us, the subject is there in a perverse role. The voyeur's subject is the object in so far as the latter's look is perturbed. And this is precisely where there is a reversal, the true subject becoming the object of the look. The same applies in exhibitionism: what the subject aims at through parading is not showing off what there is to be seen; what the subject aims at is the horror evoked in the other. Fundamentally, "The true aim of desire is the other, as constrained, beyond his involvement in the scene."[30] This is a way of saying that what counts is to hit the target: bull's-eye!

Applying this to clinical work with babies, we could say that the child needs to become a voyeur at the first stage, and then an exhibitionist at the third. I have already described how well babies can deploy their capacities as voyeurs; what remains is to outline their talents as exhibitionists. If we follow Freud and Lacan, we can see that in the fashion of the perverse subject, it is less a question for babies of showing themselves off by parading and more a question of producing an effect on the other. What babies are seeking, and the reason why they go to such lengths, is to ensure that their actions hit the bull's eye on the side of the other. This is just like the exhibitionist, who as Lacan put it, does not only seek to show off his sexual organ, but sets things up so that "just as the number two delights at being odd, the sex, or widdler, delights at being looked at".[31] It is this rejoicing in provoking something on the side of the other that is precisely what is aimed at, but which may also fail.

Failure of the third time

So what happened for Illan? He certainly did not fail to do all he could to attract our attention. He never stopped wriggling and jumping up and down on the spot. He exhausted himself playing the comic, parading with a sadly fixed smile or laugh. In a certain way, he was showing off. However, all his efforts were in vain, because he was enmeshed in an image which was stuck to his very eyes, the inverted image of his dead brother. Illan never stopped showing himself, without ever reaching his target on the side of the other.

For him, there was no third stage, except as a kind of puppet. Poor little clown, who could make his mother smile, but could never make her laugh. What was at stake, as we can see, went well beyond the place of the anti-depressant object which this little boy had taken up in relation to his mother. What was in question here was in the register of a derailment, which had not allowed the circuit of the drive to be set in motion and intertwine with narcissism. The first time of the drive was compromised because a neonatal history of extreme prematurity was accompanied by a death; in such cases the baby remains close to death, and may even die.

In this primordial stage, where the force of life has to struggle to gain the upper hand, the baby is most often encountered as the object of care-giving. More than anything else, the vital functions of such babies are considered to be paramount. The mother's preoccupations, and those of the medical team, are centred on the organic and the life drives. As we know, the paradigm of the drives is the partial sexual drives. In an encounter like this one, there is a risk that the newborn child will remain without the body being libidinised, and there is a higher risk than ever of the non-inscription of the drives.

Then there was the derailing of the second time, during which ordinary babies play with their reflection in the mirror and gain access to the symbolic. It is a necessary transition in which a baby moves on from the two-dimensional to the three-dimensional and thus in principle gains access to reality. From this point of view, both the child and the mother have to give up on imaginary omnipotence. As Bergès emphasised, "both he and his mother are mourning: he is mourning his mother, who no longer obeys him, and she is mourning his image, which has fallen, since her child has consciously become other to her".[32] But for Illan, the mirror did not have this structuring effect. In his trajectory, he had bypassed this, and risked actually going through the mirror to its other side.

So there was the derailment of the third time, which is that of psychical structuring in the course of which a subject is produced, but also the time when the subject may not be produced, as was the case for Illan.

As we can see, the inscription of the drives in the very first time has effects which condition the advent of the 'ego' during the second time. These two times thus constitute valuable and essential markers when we work with very small babies.

Thanks to the unpacking of the drives, we are able to see this absence of structuring more clearly. It is also what has allowed us to orientate our work in order for the drives to be put in place and be set in motion again, and not just in an acephalic circulation, that is, a circulation that produces no subjectivity.

Once he could be disengaged from this mortifying reflection, Illan was able to identify with a representation of himself, that is to say, an image which in some way did not entirely cover over who he was. Fundamentally, we could say that a child who sees his or her image identifies with a decoy, knotting together reality and the imaginary. This is precisely the operation of language, which articulates the thing and the word through its knotting. Thanks to this, the little child can now have access to the symbolic, with its property of being ungraspable, and he or she can also enter into the third time of the drive and pass through the order of the parade to that of the masquerade.

Notes

1   J. Lacan, '*Anxiety*', op. cit. pp. 240–1.
2   J. Lacan, '*The Four Fundamental Concepts*', op. cit. pp. 195–6.
3   S. Freud, 'Drives', op. cit. p. 130.
4   J. Lacan, '*The Four Fundamental Concepts*', p. 190.
5   H. Bouasse, *Optique et photométrie dites géometriques*, Delagrave, 1949, p. 87. Cited by J. Lacan in '*Ecrits*', op. cit. p. 564.
6   J. Lacan, '*The Seminar Book 1, Freud's Papers on Technique*' (1953–4), ed. J.-A. Miller, Cambridge University Press, 1988, p. 79.
7   M.-C. Laznik, 'Des psychanalystes qui travaillent en santé publique', op. cit. p. 93.
8   M.-C. Laznik, 'Entre depression du bébé et autisme', paper given on 27 September 2016 at Chapelle-aux-Champs as part of Formation clinique psychanalytique enfant (FCPE) at the University of Louvain.
9   J. Lacan, 'The mirror stage as formative of the I function' (1949), in '*Ecrits*', op. cit. pp. 75–81. The importance of the mirror in the process of psychical construction of babies had already been noted by Henri Wallon in 1931, but Lacan was the first to introduce it into psychoanalysis, followed by Winnicott and Dolto.
10 J. Bergès, G. Balbo, *Psychose, autisme et défaillance cognitive chez l'enfant*, Toulouse, érès, 2010, p. 32.
11 J. Lacan, '*The Four Fundamental Concepts*', op. cit. p. 193.
12 What follows here is a re-working of my papers: 'Pulsion et prématurité', *Épistoles*, No. 6, *Cliniques périnatales*, 2015, and 'Pulsion et direction de la cure chez le bébé à la lumière de la prématurité', in G. Druel, ed., *Losque le sujet paraît… Naissance du sujet et clinique des tout-petits*, Presses universitaires de Rennes, 2017.
13 Once again, this refers to the Parent and Baby Unit of Clairs Vallons, Ottignies, Belgium.

14 The test in question is the Brunet-Lézine developmental scale. It is a tool to evaluate the developmental age of babies between 2 and 30 months. It is administered to all babies on admission to and discharge from the unit, both to orientate the therapeutic work and to measure outcomes.

15 J. Lacan, '*Anxiety*', op. cit. p. 39.

16 S. Freud, 'On Narcissism', op. cit. p. 91.

17 P. de Georges, *La pulsion et ses avatars. Un concept fondamental de la psychologie*, op. cit. p. 56.

18 J. Lacan, '*The Four Fundamental Concepts*', op. cit. p. 175.

19 Ibid. p. 189.

20 Cited by P. de Georges, *La pulsion et ses avatars*, op. cit., p. 56.

21 M. Safouan, *L'échec du principe de plaisir*, Paris, Le Seuil, 1979, p. 70.

22 P. de Georges, *La pulsion et ses avatars*, op. cit. p. 56.

23 Ibid.

24 S. Freud, 'Drives', op. cit. p. 129.

25 J. Lacan, '*The Four Fundamental Concepts*', op. cit. p. 177.

26 S. Freud, 'Drives', op. cit. p. 129.

27 J. Lacan, '*The Four Fundamental Concepts*', op. cit. p. 178.

28 Ibid.

29 Ibid. p. 182.

30 Ibid.

31 Ibid. p. 194.

32 J. Bergès, G. Balbo, *Psychose, autisme et défaillance cognitive chez l'enfant*, op. cit. p. 34.

Chapter 5

The field of invocation

Marie Couvert

The invocatory drive was a discovery of Lacan's. However, it had already been at play since Freud's invention of a treatment based exclusively on speech. But Freud did not include the voice as an object of the drive. It was Lacan who noted something insistent, with an effect of inscription, in this sonorous object. From *Seminar II* onwards, he had recognised "the efficiency of speech" in the treatment.[1] In so doing, he made a radical distinction between the field of language in the unconscious and the field of communication.

Ten years later, he was to take up the voice on the basis of pure sound with its dimension of pulsation. He established that invocation imposes itself, in the same way as orality and specularity, as a factor in psychical structuration. He said, "I am filling in the gaps that Freud, surprisingly, left in his enumeration of the drives. After *making oneself seen*, I will introduce another, *making oneself heard*, of which Freud says nothing."[2] However, he told us very little about this third register, this "strange thing". He outlined very briefly how the field of invocation was distinguished from the two others by the fact that "in the field of the unconscious the ears are the only orifice that cannot be closed".[3] And he added that in "making oneself heard" there is a dimension which is resolutely aimed at the other, and the reason for this is structural. Then . . . nothing more; everything happened as if, like Freud, Lacan was passing on the baton, and it was now up to us to fill in the gaps. And this is what Alain Didier-Weill did by trying to discern a musical dimension in the pulsation of sound as an effect of attachment and of astonishment.[4]

But in *Seminar XI*, where the question of invocation arises, Lacan in a way gets straight to the point, because he refers explicitly to newborn babies. Marie-Christine Laznik, following Didier-Weill, turned her attention to the effects of sound in the encounter with babies, and she, better than anyone else, grasped what it was that Lacan intended us to understand when he introduced the voice as an object of the drive.

Let us return to the very short paragraph devoted to the invocatory drive, in which Lacan wrote that "making oneself heard goes towards the other. The reason for this is a structural one - it was important that I should mention it in passing."[5] So the voice in its acoustic dimension is addressed to the other, whereas the scopic was initially turned towards the self.

But that is not all. Laznik's genius is to have shown how Lacan's remark indicates how *the voice operates on structure*. Indeed, we shall see that well-attuned babies allow their body to resonate to the musicality of the mother. On the other hand, babies at risk of autism are precisely those who cannot easily be reached through the resonance of sound. Thus, the voice in its acoustic materiality can come to inscribe the mark of the Other in babies for whom things are going well, and make them into speaking subjects.

The percussive nature of sound in the first time of invocation evokes the inscription of an initial Bejahung. For tiny babies, the *Bejahung* transmits the acceptance of being penetrated by something coming from the Other. We may even conceive of it as "a founding psychical act of the unconscious".[6] And since *Bejahung* means affirmation, we could say that it constitutes a first 'yes' addressed by the baby to the other who summons him or her to produce it. So this inaugural 'yes' is precisely "the condition such that something exists for a subject".[7] From then on, everything unfolds as if the baby, by saying 'yes' to this pathway of the voice which comes from the other, were at the same time renouncing being nothing but him or herself, in order to bring an Other for him or herself into existence. We shall see how pivotal this is, in the direction of the treatment of certain babies, to accept something that is no less than a forcing of the Other through the voice. And this is especially true with those who find it impossible to allow themselves to be reached by playing with their body like a sound-box, because such babies are resistant to the language of the Other.

The invocatory drive can fail, just like the other drives, and these failures will have structural consequences on the development of the very young subject. So the next question concerns the conditions that govern the inscription of sonorousness for the very small speaking being.

First time: hearing

Nowadays, the vocal object is at the heart of research. In conjunction with the face, the voice has the ability to act as a powerful operator in the inscription of the bond with the other. We know, too, that the invocatory drive comes to structure that relation during the course of the first year. Clinical work with babies indeed shows that the newborn has an astonishing appetite for the voice of the Other, and that in return the latter vocalises a babble that is perfectly tailored to the baby, and encourages engagement in the exchange. What we nowadays call 'motherese' designates the maternal prosody which has the power to seduce the little one. The more recent designation of 'parentese' indicates that fathers are just as capable of producing this prosody. On the baby's side, we talk of 'jabbering' or 'babbling', which designates the newborn's language long before the appearance of vocalisation.

Lacan himself had already conceptualised the vocal exchanges between babies and their primordial others with his invention of 'lalangue'. It was a rather avant-garde way of making us understand that the newborn baby is a speaking being, a *'parlêtre'*, and that language is not reducible to emissions of meaning.[8]

More recently, Colwyn Trevarthen analysed sequences of speech between a mother and her baby, showing that motherese is the bearer of emotions that the newborn can perceive and differentiate between: the mother initiates a sentence, the baby fills in the gaps, and what is more, knows how the story ends:

MOTHER: "Come on" (pause), "come on [again]" (pause)
BABY: "Hey" "Hey"
MOTHER: "Come on" (pause), "that's clever!" "Hey-hey"
BABY: "Hey" "Hey-hey"All of this constitutes a conversation.[9]

Trevarthen describes it as "rhythmic courtesy". Marie-Christine Laznik introduced us to the characteristics of this voice that make the baby find it so delicious. The newborn has a musical appetite for vocal exchanges with the partner, mother or father. So the voice in its acoustic materiality does not fall into the category of the satisfaction of needs. The satisfaction linked to it comes from the fact that the voice is the bearer of something else, and everything unfolds as if the baby was excited by the musicality of motherese.

So what is particular about this voice that makes the baby find it so delicious? Anne Fernald, a psycholinguist, has made a study of the characteristics of motherese; she shows that it is generally situated an octave higher than normal exchanges between adults, its rhythm is slower and it contains prosodic spikes, such as a sound that 'takes off' at the end of a phrase.[10] Apparently, babies prefer ascending sounds to descending sounds, just as they prefer intonations of approval to those of disapproval.

But there is more to it; she also discovered that without their babies, mothers are less capable of producing prosodic spikes. If the mother speaks motherese less well without the presence of her child, this is because the baby has the power of awakening this particular know-how. The question then is what it is that provokes such flights of lyricism in the mother. In order to answer this question, Fernald studied other conditions in which these melodic spikes were reproduced, for example, with another adult. She discovered that it would occur in unusual situations, which would need to evoke tremendous surprise, astonishment combined with great pleasure, or very great joy. Surprise would provoke a high spike in the parent's voice, whereas pleasure would provoke a low one. "When the two occur in succession, it creates a pattern of 'hills and valleys' just like the prosody of parentese."[11] Astonishment combined with pleasure would thus produce this type of pattern of spikes. This enables us to realise the place babies occupy in their mother's psyche, if they can cause such an inflation of prosodic tonality. But at the same time we also see that newborn babies have an extraordinary appetite for the jouissance their presence triggers in the maternal other. Indeed, this caused Trevarthen to say that the baby is born with "the motive for a motive for the other".[12]

And yet some babies do not latch on to maternal prosody. I would like to pause on this question of 'failure', and on what we might try to do in order to introduce a tiny baby to the language of the Other.

Failure of the first time

Victor was a baby who cried all the time; nothing could stop him or calm him down.[13] This was clear from the very first session. He was six weeks old, sleeping in a baby chair opposite me while his mother told me how powerless she was:

> "He does nothing but cry, and he never sleeps either. I'd like someone to observe him, observe his behaviour. There's something wrong with his behaviour. There's nothing you can do to console him . . . There's something really wrong in the way I am with him and the way he is with me, I'm aware of that. He cries all the time, and when you pick him up, you could almost say he pushes you away. If you try some 'consoling man-oeuvres' [those were the mother's words, '*manoeuvres de consolation*'], it's as if he was repelling them, rejecting them . . ."

She said again, "There's something wrong with his behaviour. I need someone to tell me what's wrong with his behaviour."

At that moment, Victor started to moan with his eyes still shut, gesticulating and kicking his legs, arching his back. With his eyes still closed, he opened his mouth and started to howl. The mother continued, while looking at her son: "There he goes, he wakes up and he cries. It gets worse and worse, he 'spirals out of control', and there's no getting him back."

Victor had woken up without opening his eyes. His little fists were clenched; he was completely tensed up. He moved his pelvis and his head from side to side. He cried loudly, with his mouth wide open. The firmness of my voice calmed him down a little. But then Victor 'spiralled out of control' again, just as his mother had described to me. I had intended to carry out a Brazelton assessment.[14] But I surprised myself by doing something I would never ordinarily do. Seeing that Victor would not calm down, with the parents' permission, I allowed myself to pick him up.

Here is what I observed: I was holding a little round ball, with an enormous mouth, wide open, from which piercing screams were being emitted. His head was actively turning away from me, and his eyes, still closed, were turned towards the light.

So I experienced my first feeling of rejection for this round and rejecting head, and then, almost at the same time, a wave of sympathy for the great open mouth and the little fugitive eyes. Later on, I found myself drawing a picture of the great round ball of a head, invaded by an enormous mouth and with just two little slits for eyes. It was as if that was Victor in his entirety, in that gaping, screaming mouth, and in the two tiny slits of his eyes.

At the same time, I felt that it could not be easy to be the mother of that particular baby. I said aloud, so as to create a transferential link, "It can't be easy being the mother of a baby who cries this much." Then, holding him firmly in my arms with his face towards me, I managed to calm Victor down by making some sweeping vertical vestibular movements. He then went into a state known as the 'alert state',[15] and I tried to begin administering items of the test bearing on orientation, in order to begin to work in the relational sphere. I started with the rattle, in other words with a stimulus that was both auditory and visual, hoping he would latch on to it. Victor repelled this stimulation, turning away in a state of agitation. It was too much for him. I realised that he had a very low threshold of tolerance, so I tried to find the upper limit of his tolerance: holding him firmly in my arms, making vestibular movements, and offering continuous vocalisation. I then observed how unbearable the unpredictability of the slightest movement was for him, and how fragile his body was. I commented to the parents that he was hypersensitive to his environment, that is to say, to sounds, to light, to movements and to touch.

I gave up trying to continue observation using test items aimed at motricity, because I anticipated that this would have an effect on Victor that would be too disturbing. I tried to keep the stimulation just close to his threshold of tolerance, but neither my holding him nor my voice succeeded in getting him to engage. His eyes were still closed as he turned his face and looked away from me with impressive determination. I became concerned. It took time, more than half an hour, with a stable situation offered by being held in my arms, by a sweeping and continuous movement, and above all by my conviction that he had the capacity to emerge from this withdrawn state, for Victor to give a tiny sign that he recognised the presence of an other. Very gently, with his eyes still shut, he turned his face towards me, and I began to speak differently to him. I would like to unpack what I mean by 'differently'. The first image that came to me, once I took a little distance from it by drawing it, was of a big circle for the face, and an only slightly smaller circle to represent the mouth.

In my eyes, this baby was nothing but a screaming, gaping hole. This meant he was very far from being "*His Majesty, The Baby*", as Freud put it. And doubtless his mother felt the same. All the while, as I was trying to calm her son down, she kept on producing a flood of fixed and negative images: "You see how he screams, that's all he knows how to do, and he never sleeps, either, well, only 'micro-sleeps', he'll never stop . . ."

In fact, as soon as I saw how Victor cut himself off, I understood that he was trying to escape from something. At that moment, he became someone other than just the crying baby. He became a baby who was highly capable of telling me that he had at all costs to avoid something, and I had no doubt that the something was his mother's words of disappointment and her tensed-up face.[16]

We could say that at this precise moment the operation of 'Bouasse's schema' had succeeded: the flowers had arrived in the vase, and Victor was now glorified. I think he noticed the glorification in my voice, because all of a sudden my voice began to give out prosodic spikes with the requisite amount of surprise and amazement. Victor was not unaware of this, and nor was his mother, because at this point she wanted to pick him up herself . . . So I put Victor on her lap, his feet pointing towards her belly; they looked at each other. His mother tried to say a few words to him, but she seemed ill at ease, and her fragility became terribly pronounced as she found herself face-to-face with him. So again I did something I never normally do: I sat down beside her, put my arms around her, and asked her what she would really like to say to her little boy. She dissolved into tears, and in a completely different voice, quite deep this time, finally managed to say, "It's so complicated for both of us!" Victor's eyes were now wide open, his mouth opened into an 'o'-shape, as if to speak; he was completely present for his mother who, deeply moved, said some tender words to him which I had not heard her say before. She was speaking motherese to him.

An encounter had taken place. Concurrently, for the first time in my experience of work with babies, and when Victor had only been alive for six weeks, I suspected very early signs of autism. His hypersensitivity, his undif-ferentiated rejections, the refusal of all contact, the tenacious and persistent staring at the light with his eyes half-closed, were flashing signals which screamed: 'Emergency!' Because there certainly is an emergency and an absolute need to do something with such babies, and it was an emergency insisting that someone went to rescue Victor from the predicament he was in.

During the following sessions, I noticed that there was one scenario, always exactly the same, which repeated itself. Each time, the mother would start by speaking of a slight improvement and then a litany of complaints would gush forth from her, and Victor, echoing her, would start crying.

Each time, I would work to provide a calming and soothing setting for Victor, but also for his mother, and my voice would eventually make contact with him. However, as his mother bitterly complained, what happened in the sessions was not replicated at home. "I want so much for him to be like that with us at home, like he is here with you", she said to me. "While he's here, he manages to calm down. You find a way to calm him down." This mother was quite right, the only thing I could manage to do was calm him down!

I must have been kidding myself by thinking that I had been present at the initiation of the first stage of the circuit of the drive. Certainly there had been a moment of encounter, but it had only been a fleeting one. I had to face the evidence: things were not holding together. Nothing seemed to be becoming inscribed from one session to the next. Each time it felt as if we were starting from scratch.

What was it that was not functioning? "A voice.is not assimilated, but incorporated", Lacan explained.[17] That is to say, in order to inscribe itself, the voice has to follow the path of identification. This is precisely what had not happened for this baby. What is more, Victor was already showing signs of agitation, and would start to scream. "Off he goes again, spiralling out of control", the mother would say, watching her baby. It occurred to me that he was not a cry-baby but a scream-baby!

Lacan, rather surprisingly, defined autistic subjects as 'verbose'.[18] This means we have to interpret their cries and screams quite differently. These vocal outpourings, which we would all like to stop, are unbearable because they are addressed to no-one. So it was up to me to make something of them. And it was then, having realised this, that, to my own astonishment, I heard myself saying to him, "Stop!" *[English in the original]* in a very firm voice. He was surprised, looked at me while making a little face, slightly aghast, and I then told him that 'no', he did not need to scream like that, he could find another way to say it.

He calmed down, breathed, pushed out his lips as if to say something, and then his lips made an o-shape, and he made a sound. With amazement and enthusiasm, I said to him: "Yes, that's right, you can say it another way." His mother could not get over it, because until then Victor had never produced any babble at all, which ordinarily signals the inscription of the second time of the invocatory drive. In the sessions that followed, I was surprised to learn that Victor was now jabbering and making musical sounds. The 'theatre of the mouth', as D. Meltzer[19] so beautifully called it, was now in place, and I could watch Victor jabbering with his mother.

Let us pause here for a moment to understand what had taken place. We saw that maternal prosody had the power to stop Victor's screaming. This had only been possible when I was overcome by moments of genuine surprise and pleasure. He was then riveted by my lips for a while, and this had the power to calm him down. Could we read this as the operation of a primary *Bejahung*? Nothing is less certain, because nothing became inscribed in the sense of an incorporation. We could say that Victor looked at the sounds I produced without swallowing them. In other words, he could not feed himself with them. From this point of view, it seemed to me that motherese, while being a necessary condition for the engagement of the drive, is perhaps not a sufficient one. But all at once, I found myself confronted with yet another enigma. How can we account for the fact that some babies manage to allow themselves to be caught up in maternal prosody, and others do not?

This led me to think about the relationship between the voice as object, and jouissance. Let us consider the sounds Victor made: a scream has something specific about it which, still, falls short of being a sign. It is, in fact, the acknowledgement of receipt on the part of the Other which gives it meaning. In other words, the scream is asking to be taken up in the network of signifiers. And it is precisely there that this baby was resisting: he refused to yield to the jouissance of language. Nothing of his scream managed to lodge itself in the emptiness of the Other, which would have allowed him to become inscribed in a primordial identification with the Other. But in order to become inscribed in the language of the Other, in other words, in a jouissance which is not merely closed in on itself or solely autoerotic, it needs to be marked by prohibition. This is what occurs in well-adjusted babies when they are caught up in the dynamic of desire.

We have seen that it is because mothers do not only respond strictly at the level of need, and suppose the existence of something else in their babies, that those babies can have access to the dynamic of desire. We see this each time a baby is captivated by the mother's melodic utterance rather than by the bottle. If babies can suck in and relish the mother's words, it is only because there is something like a 'non-response', a primordial refusal to oppose the side of primary satisfaction, which in turn rests upon the supposition of a subject in the baby and allows for the inscription of the symbolic and access to the language of the Other.

I now wondered if my intervention from a rather more paternal position, spoken in the form of a prohibition, might not have had the effect of freeing Victor from a satisfaction that was not connected with the Other. Perhaps it had emerged to mark a cut which enabled him to move away from a closed circuit of jouissance, supported by the death drive, which is what we see affecting many autistic children.

In other words, could this operation have provided the foundation for a subject? It seemed to me that one could perhaps read in it a relation of primordial identification in the sense of the 'single trait' conceptualised by Freud, and which constitutes the absolute minimum in terms of a relation to the other. Freud designated this trait as the most primitive experience of differentiation from the object. It is, in a certain sense, what impels the emergence of the *Bejahung*. In any case, Lacan took up this notion and made it an essential part of his concept of structure. Identification based on a single trait, in this case my voice bearing a prohibition, would then have a function of differentiation based on a principle of negativity. It is an operation though which a subject is constrained to pass via an other in order to come into being. The 'single trait' would then provide punctuation, introducing the mark of a before and an after. For a baby like Victor, who defended himself in an autistic way, this constraint enabled him to move on from being one who "screams all by himself" to one who "cries for an other". What was at stake here was quite apt, because the scream, which was now addressed to someone, engaged the child in the circuit of the drives, which is something all autistic babies resist. It is not surprising that this structuring trait operates on the basis of the paternal function.

Here I am questioning the hypothesis that the paternal voice, in its sonorous materiality, has a role in the inscription of the 'single trait' in subjects like Victor. Because, *post hoc*, I noticed that I had supported my act using a voice which placed more emphasis on the consonants. If we take a closer look, the 'Stop!' I had challenged Victor with contained no fewer than three consonants out of four letters. And among the hardest consonants, we find the occlusive, of which 't' is the most powerful in the French language.

The field of the characteristics and function of the paternal voice as object remains relatively unexplored, but I was able to find some suggestions in the work of Anne Alvarez[20] and Geneviève Haag.[21] Both authors emphasise that the paternal voice is relatively laden with the sound of consonants, giving it a more serious, harder and stronger timbre. On the other hand, vocalised sounds are associated more with maternal prosody. The articulation of consonants also introduces cuts in the continuity of vocalised sounds, and this, according to Haag, can be attributed to the 'masculine/paternal'[22] model.

My vocal interjection, with its cutting resonance, may have allowed something to fall into place for Victor, the matrix of identification, or the operation of a 'single trait', offering him an opening to the Other. This is a hypothesis, but one which in any case invites us to think differently about our encounters with these children. Such babies challenge the analyst to work in a different way. They lead us to explore positions which are quite alien to our practice, and to occupy a place in the transference that Rene Diatkine, speaking of mothers, referred to as "a necessary madness".

Up to that point I had never suddenly picked up a newborn baby, I had never made a drawing of a baby, and I had never put my arms around one of the mothers. But above all, I had never dared to think that I might help a baby out of a withdrawn state by using a harsh voice.

Second time: listening to oneself

During the second time, babies listen to themselves. They delight in producing sound-objects: lallations and vocalisations. This activity of pure pleasure, which has an autoerotic function, is not, however, in a closed circuit. Autoeroticism, as we know, does not mean indifference to the other: quite the opposite, Lacan told us, because babies during the second stage of invocation devote themselves to listening again and again to the sounds which have been addressed to them by the other. We may thus hypothesise that by producing these sounds, children are imitating the prosodic spikes of motherese. Indeed babies are perfectly capable of reproducing precisely the same frequency of sound as that of the mother's voice. The production of sounds by babies would then have an effect of presence, of making the lost object of the maternal voice resonate again. In doing this, the second time of invocation would be the moment when the baby first demonstrates a version of the *Fort-Da*, a long time before the acquisition of a coded language.

The game of *Fort-Da* is a Freudian conceptualisation of a primary activity of symbolisation by the psychical apparatus. In *Beyond the Pleasure Principle,* Freud shared with us an observation of his grandson Ernst: "At the age of one and a half he could say only a few comprehensible words; he could also make use of a number of sounds which expressed a meaning intelligible to those around him."[23] This child, Freud told us, had the habit of throwing every small object that he grasped away from him. At the same time he made an expressive sound full of interest and satisfaction: a long, sonorous *o-o-o-o*, which, according to both the child's mother and Freud the observer, was not a mere interjection, but meant *fort*, 'away, gone'.[24] And Freud observed that indeed, his grandson used his toys exclusively to play at '*fortsein*', 'being away, being gone'. And then one day the child found a cotton reel with a thread wound around it, and began throwing it down with great dexterity, in order to see it disappear; he would accompany this action with his *o-o-o-o*, full of meaning; then he would pull the cotton reel by the thread out of the cot, greeting its reappearance with a joyful *da* ('*here*').[25] The game Ernst was playing was making something go away and come back, and Freud interpreted this as a renunciation of the satisfaction of the drive. This renunciation now became coupled with a scenario involving a sound, actively produced by the child, accompanying the departure and return of something he would have liked to keep close to him.

This metaphorising activity is precisely what is lacking in children at risk of psychosis. For such children, there is no possibility of symbolising absence; young psychotic subjects do not recognise the *fort*, the presence of an absence is indifferent to them, to the extent that for them, "there is nothing but da-da-da . . .".[26]

We can see that the second time of invocation can be crucial for structure. It then becomes clear how important it is to monitor it very early on. When well-adjusted babies delight in motherese, they are telling us two things. On the one hand, they have managed to let themselves be struck physically by the voice of an other while taking account of the presence of the latter. And on the other hand, they show that they can also deal with absence, being capable very early on of transforming it by making it present through the sounds they produce themselves. This second time is in some way the guarantor of the engagement with the symbolic, and this is why it constitutes a structural pivot, something which Lacan insisted upon.

In clinical work with babies, the absence of the second stage, whether in the form of poverty of production of sounds, or, on the contrary, of an uninterrupted sound in the form of incessant screaming, should always elicit close attention on the part of the clinician.

Failure of the second time

The hypothesis that the second time of invocation emerges from a knotting with the activation of the *Fort-Da* means that we need to examine the positions of the parents. While presence is primordial during the first time, we can say that it is the alternation of presence and absence of the maternal other which forms the basis of the second time, and the emergence of the *Fort-Da*. In other words, for the child to enter the autoerotic stage, it is necessary for the mother, having established her presence, to be able to absent herself. Because offering only the modality of presence means that the baby is never invited to come to terms with absence. It is then impossible for him or her to access the representation of presence by creating a scenario of absence.

Maya was a baby who screamed, but nothing could make her babble. She had just arrived in the unit, aged three weeks. I chose to carry out a short version of the Brazelton scale, because it shows rather well how the mother is making her presence felt for the baby.

During the test, Maya showed several times how quickly she became saturated. Each time I handled her, her mother would intervene with her voice, or through touching her: she would talk over me, push herself into the baby's field of vision, stroke her little head, her arms, her feet . . . It was all far too much for Maya, her threshold of tolerance was reached very quickly, and she expressed irritation each time it was exceeded. Everything happened as if all my efforts were being replicated by those of her mother, and immediately became intrusive; so I had to pause from time to time, and eventually gave up administering the test.

I am now going to demonstrate and present in 'dramatic' form the exchanges that Maya found so unbearable. I tried to get across to her mother that we needed to try very hard to interact with Maya in a way that did not upset her. I explained that she was an extremely sensitive little baby, and possibly even rather fragile, but that she could certainly scream powerfully and tenaciously, and that we should not disturb her if she wanted to be left alone. But there was no way I could persuade the mother to desist from being continuously present in an intrusive way. I was just on the point of stopping the test in order to let the baby recuperate, and for the mother to quietly observe how she was faring. But the mother grabbed her daughter's foot, and pushed on her bootee without any regard for her, and then grabbed the other foot, causing Maya to start screaming. This sequence is a paradigm of the mother-daughter relationship in this case. What is it that would cause a mother to keep 'pestering' her baby when the child never stops telling her, "Just leave me alone"? There was a kind of haste to intervene, and more generally to always be there for the child. No doubt there is an element of the need to feel that one is a parent. It appeared here in a transitive form;[27] the mother needed to feel that she was the mother of this particular child by constantly poking and prodding her. For her, in a certain way, this helped in the inscription of 'being a mother'. She then attributed the need to her baby. There was no doubt in her mind that Maya just loved being pestered in this way. For the mother, it guaranteed that she could recognise herself as a mother who responded perfectly to her baby's needs.

Everything took place as if the maternal function in its attributive and transitive aspects, as Bergès[28] and Cullere-Crespin[29] described them, was utterly debased. This debasement bore on the fact that the mother could not see that the baby was saying something different. And the baby would just have to make the adjustment and adapt to the mother. Indeed, Maya now protested by screaming to be picked up all the time, and then carried around or rocked. This was the baby's own creation, her own discovery in a sense, in order to adjust to her mother: offering to be there for her all the time, too; the price she paid was to be nothing but an object to be picked up and rocked back and forth.

If we go back to the kind of scene described above, it is at the point where the baby continues to scream or howl when the mother decides it is time to feed him or her, or in Maya's case to pester her, that it is necessary to move to the paternal position. "The paternal function comes to support the alterity of the baby",[30] because in the encounter with his newborn child, the father does not yet know who he or she is; so he asks the question. Where the mother acts transitively, and attributes the contents of her own thoughts to the baby, the father questions and opens up another field. The maternal other makes statements such as, "you are" or "you want" this or that; correspondingly, the paternal other asks questions: "Who are you?" and "What do you want?" In the primordial link to the other, the baby needs to be able to benefit from both positions, and a well-adjusted parent would be able to incarnate both sides, maternal and paternal, in turn. But the turning towards a paternal position is possible only if the other can allow him- or herself to be 'de-completed', "or to put it in terms of the *Fort-Da*, if the other goes away and comes back".[31] This is precisely what Maya's mother was resisting, by being there all the time.

So what about Maya's father, what was his presence like during the sessions?

When I saw them for the first session, Maya was crying. Although she was being held by her father, it did not seem enough to soothe her. So he changed the way he was carrying her: he turned his daughter to face him, giving her plenty of points to lean on, and rocked her with a sweeping motion, up and down, up and down, trying to soothe her. Then he complemented his action with his voice, modulating it perfectly. It was a magnificent prosody, full of the spikes proper to motherese, and I was immediately impressed by this father's mothering capacities. And it did have an effect on his daughter, who stopped screaming, looked at her father, and literally drank in his words, forgetting she was hungry. I thought at the time that I was witnessing 'live' the putting into place of the first stage of the circuit of the invocatory drive. Maya appeared to have a highly competent father who was capable of introducing her into the symbolic field of the invocatory link. He continued his vocal exchanges with her, and Maya remained riveted by her father's chanting. Now I was the spectator at a lovely ballet performance: a little baby girl was being swung continuously with perfect, supple movements, to the rhythm of a never-ending, magnificent melody. And yet I surprised myself by wondering whether it would all come to an end fairly soon. And indeed, the father stopped so that he could put her on his knees to give her a bottle. At that moment, Maya cut off completely, her gaze wandered from him, completely empty and absent. One could have argued that she was having a break so that she could take in the liquid, but all of a sudden she had deprived herself of the possibility of having any sort of repletion other than an organic one. The father was aware of this, he was worried, and asked me several times what his daughter was looking at. I suggested that Maya might need a little break. So he modulated his voice, and I listened as he spoke to her much more softly; this allowed the baby to relax, but only for a short time.

Because as soon as the bottle was finished, he started to carry her around again, walking and strolling, with the same vertical swinging movements, in time to the sonorous rhythm of his soliloquy. All this time, Maya did nothing, said nothing, was completely passive; she was there but not there. And I myself felt almost drunk listening to this vocal force-feeding.

I noticed that the father was occupying a maternal position, mirroring that of the mother.

I had realised that each time Maya showed interest in anything, the mother would cut short her enthusiasm by bringing her attention back to herself: singing, waving her hands around, to make the child look at her. In so doing, she actively annulled every attempt her baby made to show some initiative. The father did not intrude on Maya in the same register, but he never stopped carrying her and stuffing her with words. Fundamentally, it was the 'never-ending' aspect of mothering that had been displaced and taken up by the father. Father and mother were occupying exactly the same position, both of them being too 'present' for the little girl.

My aim, then, was to work towards disengaging Maya from being trapped in a maternal position which was never interrupted by a paternal one. In other words, it was a question of supporting the father so that he could articulate the two positions himself.

To guide me, I used the fact that there was an established circuit of the drive between Maya and her father. She could calm down in his arms, she could become attached to his prosody, and she would look deep into his eyes. So it looked as if, provided we took care, it would be possible to eroticise all three registers of the drive. There was no lack of a certain quality of presence, a certain maternal know-how, in this father; I felt I could bank on him.

I recalled that he had introduced himself to me by saying that he wanted to be there for his daughter, so I asked him to unpack what he meant by 'there'. He immediately spoke about his own childhood; he was the eldest sibling, but when he was four years old his father left the family, leaving him alone with his mother. From that time on, he remembered having to get up very early to pick fruit, and going off to sell it. He said that his parents were not present for him in the way he now wanted to be present for Maya. Now we could better understand why the 'there' that circumscribed his paternal presence was so overwhelming. We agreed to work so that he could be there for his daughter, but in a different way. Because being there also requires a capacity to withdraw, and I offered to help her father achieve this. I would support everything that had an effect of presence, everything that had an effect of encounter between him and Maya.

During the sessions, moments of true presence, which had the effect of animating Maya, alternated with periods of overstimulation and 'force-feeding'. Sometimes the father would very subtly notice that Maya was looking at something somewhere else, and would pick up on it. One day he noticed that she was looking intently at some little wooden figures sitting on the window-sill; he stopped what he was doing, put Maya down on the mat, and brought them to her, saying to her: "Oh, you were looking at these, maybe you've already played with them in Madame Couvert's office, is this what you want?"

He gave her the toys, animating the game energetically, making the little figures jump over each other, and inviting Maya to do the same. She then watched her father while she played, and when she saw that he was sometimes looking behind her, she turned her head and saw herself in the mirror. She was very interested in this, and her father was happy to see her move so that she could see herself better. He commented: "That's Maya, Maya and Daddy, yes, that's Maya and her Daddy." Then the father turned towards me and said, "There's a lot more going on now than when I'm holding her! It's much more lively like this!"

What had happened in this sequence was that the father had moved away from Maya, he had noticed what his daughter was interested in, and had supported her desire. This is exactly the kind of action that is expected from the paternal position. This father now knew how to do it, and we can also see that the discourse addressed to his daughter which encouraged this activity had the structure of questioning, which also characterises the paternal position.

What is particular about the interrogative sentence is that it includes the hypothesis of an answer, and therefore the hypothesis of a speaking subject. In any case, Maya made no mistake: in reply, she babbled, which corresponds exactly to the second stage in the register of invocation.

Third time: making oneself heard

There is no doubt that we need to take stock of the fact that when Lacan introduced the invocatory drive, he did so on the basis of *making oneself heard*, in other words, he emphasised the third time. What he essentially told us is, "After the business of 'making oneself seen', there's a 'making oneself heard'." What is it that is concentrated in this '*making oneself . . .*'? Lacan's answer to this was: all the activity of the drive. But be careful, this activity cannot be summed up as being simply the action of turning from passivity to activity! Nor is it a question of reciprocity where the subject, having listened, would be impelled to make him- or herself heard. "Does it not seem that the drive, in this turning inside out represented by its pocket, invaginating through the erogenous zone, is given the task of seeking something that, each time, responds in the Other?"[32] What Lacan was trying to indicate, and inviting us to explore, are the effects on the Other of this movement of calling.

Put another way, what is at play in this third time of *making oneself heard* can be grasped not so much from the baby's perspective but through the effects provoked in the Other. And the thing that Lacan singled out from among those effects was the dimension of the call. There would thus be something in screams, in tears or howls, or on the other hand in silences, in the absence of sound, which should be understood and treated as a call to the Other.

Would this something be what causes the transition from *making oneself heard* on the baby's side, to a C*he vuoi?* on the side of the Other? It is precisely in this transition that the subject emerges. Which made it clear to Lacan that "the subject, *in initio*, begins in the locus of the Other, in so far as it is there that the first signifier emerges".[33] In other words, it is the resonance in the primordial other of the *making oneself heard* that causes something of the subject to emerge in the baby. So it is in the acknowledgement of receipt that the third time of the invocatory drive plays itself out. But then, what is the status of this resonance on the side of the other that is required for something of the subject to be produced?

Here we find ourselves at the heart of "the original articulation of the signifier and the real".[34] Following Freud, Alain Didier-Weill tried to represent this inaugural point of knotting, which is so hard to conceptualise. Freud had used the example of the magic writing pad, with a stylus scratching a line in the wax. But Didier-Weill noted quite rightly that this model is based on an active-passive polarity which is not appropriate. Not because, as he said, it referred to the sexual, but because it is not appropriate to consider the action of the 'stylus' of the primordial other, on the one hand, and on the other, the passivity of the baby reduced to the status of a wax tablet.

He also raised the question of who started it. "Was the wax tablet waiting for the stylus, or was the stylus looking for the wax?"[35] How can we escape this dualism? This is where Alain Didier-Weill invites us to think of resonance as a third function. What led him to formulate this hypothesis was Freud's work on jokes. The flash of wit, which often takes its speaker unawares, does not fail to cause a certain momentary destabilisation in the one who intercepts it. And Freud analysed this destabilisation into two stages: bewilderment and illumination. In the first stage, the incongruity of the words brings the listener up short, the process of linkage in the signifying chain is challenged, leaving them in a state of stupefaction, of bewilderment, as Freud told us. The second stage ensues, where the incongruous verbal creation generates a new meaning, which jumps out like a spark. Something which was not there before emerges in this moment of illumination. *Fiat lux*; the light is revelatory. Let us take the famous example of Heinrich Heine's *famillionaire*, reported by Freud: the person who heard it was expecting to be introduced into the signifying logic of the chain of 'familiar' or 'millionaire'.[36] During the first stage, the convergence of the two chains appears to be a mistake, it sounds odd in the receiver's ears; this is the moment of bewilderment. Then the second stage reveals itself like a second drum-beat, and bewilderment gives way to illumination. A new word springs forth, something which had not reached us before finally resonates, to give a different music. This music is exactly what was latent in the mind of the person who enunciated it, but it is only when it strikes the other that it can be heard by the former. What has finally resonated will not be without its effects, and we shall see both the one who created the joke and the listener overcome by shared laughter.

Applying this in clinical work with babies, Marie-Christine Laznik invites us to treat the sounds made by babies just as we would treat jokes.[37] When a mother speaks with her baby, and the latter responds with any sound whatever, the mother invests the sound libidinally. To her ears, it is not just a noise; she hears something well beyond it. And when the little child comes out with "ma-ma-ma", the mother is initially flabbergasted: what a proclamation! And then it resonates, she starts to believe in it, and now hears something else. And the baby, delighted, listens to the mother's interpretation, who says: "Yes, you said mummy, oh yes, you can talk already!" This maternal madness is indispensable in order to allow the baby to *make itself heard.* Indeed, through doing this, the mother initiates the operation through which "the signifier will introduce into the developing human a subtraction of being which will be generative of structure"[38]

As we shall see, failures of the third time are precisely defects in the resonance on the side of the other, an absence of being bewildered and illuminated.

Failure of the third time

The case of Mary is exemplary; she taught me never to give up on what babies offer us to understand and interpret: it was she who introduced me to the power of the scream.

Mary was four months old. She was lying on her back, enveloped in a 'sleep-wrap'. Her mother and I were sitting on the floor beside her, in my office in the unit with which Mary and her mother were quite familiar. In front of me was a baby girl who was looking fixedly at me, but without initiating any movement. As usual, she lay there without budging, while staring into my eyes without interruption. I started speaking to her, and then I saw her gradually opening her mouth, as if she was mirroring mine. I said to her, "Oh, yes, I can see that you want to say something; I'm listening to you!" And then Mary, whose voice I had almost never heard, produced a melodious 'babble' for me, in a tonality identical to mine. We were in the same octave. Then her vocalisations became more guttural. I tried to respond to her in the same tone, but Mary did not seem to like this, and babbled over my voice; the tessitura became sharper and more and more inaccessible. She made no opportunity for me to join in with her again, and left no space for me to respond to her with words. It was no longer a conversation, but rather a tirade or a litany that had no end. I commented on this extraordinary vocal capacity to her mother. And because her mother was a law student, I went so far as to make a joke, glorifying the baby by imagining her in the future as a great lawyer. For a long time, Mary continued to vocalise, while I continued to watch her in astonishment. And then suddenly, tears appeared in her eyes, she wriggled, and burst out crying.

What had happened?

At first, I assumed that this sudden change had come about because of the considerable energy she had used up in wanting to speak. But I was resisting! It was only two days later that I understood, when I thought again about this sequence of events, and recalled Mary's history. What was it that I was resisting? Doubtless I was doing so through failing to offer her an unconscious that was capable of being the locus of undesirable images and emotions.

Mary had spent nine months in the womb without her mother being able to think about her. Sent from Africa by her family, this young woman had been instructed to do brilliantly in her studies before returning to her home country. Mary's arrival ruined this project, and left the young woman with a symbolic debt. Once her unexpected birth had occurred, Mary lived with her mother for six weeks, first in the maternity unit and then at a home, when the decision was made that a placement in a foster home seemed the only possible solution. Then Mary found herself separated from her mother and placed in a day nursery. However, only a few days later, and contrary to all expectations, her mother came to see her. She now came to see her every day. So another plan was embarked upon, and a few weeks later they arrived together at the unit where I work.

And in my encounter with Mary, I had as it were obliterated the time of the placement in the nursery. I had wanted to hear the desire to speak and the pleasure of speaking, in the sound of her voice and in her attempt to form words; but I created an impasse, so that what she wanted to say could not be heard.

I have no doubt that this was because what she wanted to 'say' bore on her abandonment. Yet she had spared no effort to signify this to me when she stared at me. Surely she had been trying to make me understand how unbearable the separation had been. But that had not worked, and so she had had to scream it at me; and even then I was deaf. So finally she had had to cry about it to communicate. When I look back, I think that her screams and her tears were demonstrations of rebuttal in the face of a misunderstanding.

While recent research shows that babies have an extraordinary appetite for conversation, and are highly capable of producing a babble that is perfectly adapted to provoke an exchange, Mary put all her energy into interrupting what I had erroneously interpreted as a conversation. She regulated the tonality of her voice, threw herself into an unending vocalisation which left no further space for an exchange, and screamed out something which I later identified as a rejection. Recognising this rejection embodied in her vocal gestures did not fail to cause a certain wavering on my part. But I think that it was a price worth paying for the shift in knowledge which occurred as a result. I found that I was obliged to let go of my preconceptions, and give up my usual points of reference. The scream, the guttural tessitura pushed to its extreme, the willpower behind an endless, uninterrupted articulation could then appear to me as the singular invention which Mary, while still only a very small baby, had initiated in order to make me hear what I later interpreted as a misunderstanding.

What was at play in the sequence of events was an active rejection, a negation of any possible reciprocity. Mary reversed the signs which usually weave and create a bond, in order to pull it apart and refuse it. The remarkable thing here is that we can see how very young babies are capable of modifying the aim of their relational capacities – jabbering, vocalisations, babble in order to avoid, or even rebuff, any exchange.

Acknowledging this rejection in the form of her screams was, I believe, an indispensable condition for this baby to be able to move into the third time of 'making herself heard'. And we should also bear in mind the fact that the inability to recognise this act of rejection could in some sense have intensified the mother's difficulties in adjusting to her, and left her child prey to an Other who could neither identify her needs nor respond to them. Because her mother and I were able to grasp what they were retroactively, and work with them, something of a truth and a certain degree of knowledge regarding the baby was able to find an echo and be taken up in the interaction. If that had not happened, there would have been a risk of leaving the child in a state of extreme solitude, even of abandonment, depriving her of the presence of another who could come to her aid. This led me to reconsider my position as analyst. This sequence of events, deciphered in the light of what causes us to 'interpret' a baby, seemed to illustrate the need, in our work with babies, to focus on specific traits, as Lacan emphasised when he invited us to work with whatever we find is offered to us.[39] The question then arises as to what is actually available to us when we work with babies. From this point of view, "differentiating behaviours, describing a scream, isolating phonemes, are among the means at our disposal to determine a treatment of *lalangue* tailored to the child, in order to insert him or her in a sequence which can make sense of them".[40] At the same time, this shows the obligation, which is always there in the field of the analyst, to rid oneself of knowledge, or the semblance of knowledge, and in this very particular work with tiny babies, that also means separating oneself from any ideology about bonding.

We might say, then, that the first stage of my interpretation testified to a position that was still trammelled by that knowledge, and Mary paid the price for it, 'abandoned' as she was to the 'discourse of the Master'. But that is not

all: Miller said that "the child is not deceived as to the nature of this semblance of knowledge", and it seemed to me that this is exactly what Mary was
showing us.[41] When she insisted with her screams and her tears, she was
surely making me understand in a glaringly obvious way that she did not
want anything to do with that semblance of knowledge.

And ultimately, as Miller points out, if the analyst has to be on the side of
the subject, in other words, of what is being said whether it be Victor's howls,
Maya's tears, or Mary's screams, we have to take these bodily events as a
production, an act of some sort, through which something of the subject
manifests itself.

Fundamentally, in order for Mary's scream not to be reduced to a mere discharge or emission of raw sound, for this scream to actually resonate, to "turn
the cry into a call", and *make itself heard* as something that has meaning, an
other had to be put into the position of being able to receive it.[42]

The curious thing is that this position in which the analyst should be able
to set aside any knowledge and create the space for whatever invention the
subject can come up with, does not mean that the analyst should know
nothing. It requires at the very least a kind of know-how capable of spotting
the traits in the tiny child that present themselves insistently, and treating
them in such a way that they are elevated to the level of language.

It seems to me that this can also shed new light on what goes on in the
treatment of adults. The way a mother treats the productions of her newborn
baby, being first amazed and then delighted, to the point of causing these
precious inventions to pour forth, might teach us how to deal with the productions of our analysands, in order to give them the status of creations that
are beyond any norm. Once again, working clinically with babies opens up
the field of working with adults.

Notes

1 J. Lacan. 'The Seminar Book 2, The Ego in Freud's Theory and in the Technique of
   Psychoanalysis' (1954–5), ed. J.-A. Miller, Cambridge University Press, 1988.
2 J. Lacan, 'The Four Fundamental Concepts', op. cit. p. 195.
3 Ibid.
4 A. Didier-Weill, Un mystère plus lointain que l'inconscient, Paris, Flammarion,
   2010, pp. 79–80.
5 J. Lacan, 'The Four Fundamental Concepts', op. cit. p. 195.
6 A. Didier-Weill, Un mystère plus lointain que l'inconscient, op. cit. p. 14.
7 J. Lacan, 'Seminar Book 1', op. cit. p. 58.
8 J. Lacan, 'The Seminar Book 23, The Sinthome' (1975–6), ed. J.-A. Miller, Cambridge, Polity, 2016.
9 Analytic case presented in a paper given at the 2 Journée de la WAIMH Franco-
   phone, 18 June 2010, on the theme of 'New clinical practices. Some questions of
   theory?'
10 A. Fernald, T. Simon, 'Expended intonation contours in mothers' speech to newborns', Developmental Psychology, No. 20, 1984, pp. 104–13.

11 M.-C. Laznik, 'La prosodie aves les bébés à risque d'autisme', in B. Touati, F. Joly, M.-C. Laznik, eds, *Langage, voix et parole dans l'autisme*, Paris, Puf, 2007, p. 192.

12 C. Trevarthen, K. Aitken, 'Infant intersubjectivity: research, theory, and clinical applications', *Journal of Child Psychology and Psychiatry*, 42, 2001, pp. 3–48.

13 Here I am re-examining a published case, 'La place de l'objet vocal dans la construction du lien', op. cit. pp. 143–51.

14 T. B. Brazelton and J. K. Nugent, *Neonatal Behavioral Assessment Scale* (NBAS), Cambridge University Press, 1975. This is a developmental scale for newborns aged 0–2 months. The administration of the test activates three systems operative in the baby: those of habituation, motricity and relationship. The way the results are interpreted aims to identify tendencies which constitute defences for the baby, while respecting the particularities of each baby. The test is administered in a place where transference is operative, facilitating self-expression in the baby.

15 T.B. Brazelton describes six states of arousal in the newborn, which range from deep sleep (State 1) to a state of paroxysmal wakefulness marked by screaming and crying (State 6). Between these two extremes, he describes light sleep (State 2); drowsy or semi-dozing (State 3); alert (State 4), which is the state where the baby is most receptive to relational interactions, and eyes open (State 5). Brazelton considered these six states as six ways of being in the world for the baby, and insisted on the baby's own capacity to regulate them.

16 Nowadays it is widely recognised that these babies have extreme hypersensitivity and a degree of receptivity to the slightest expression of negativity (whether in the voice or in the facial expression), that far exceeds the norm: an anxious or hopeless tone of voice, the merest frown, tiny wrinkles appearing at the corners of a mouth.

17 J. Lacan, '*Anxiety*', op. cit. p. 277.

18 J. Lacan, 'Geneva Lecture on the Symptom' (1975), *Analysis*, 1, 1989, pp. 7–26.

19 D. Meltzer et al. *Explorations in Autism*, London, Karnac, 1975.

20 A. Alvarez, "Trouvez la bonne longueur d'ondes: les outils de communication avec les enfants autistes', in B. Touati, F. Joly, M.-C. Laznik, eds, *Langage, voix et parole dans l'autisme*, op. cit. pp. 239–60.

21 G. Haag, 'Réflexions sur quelques particularités des émergences de langage chex les enfants autistes', in B. Touati, F. Joly, M.-C. Laznik, eds, *Langage, voix et parole dans l'autisme*, op. cit. pp. 145–65.

22 Ibid. p. 162.

23 S. Freud, '*Beyond the Pleasure Principle*' (1920), Standard Edition 18, p. 14.

24 Ibid. p.15.

25 Ibid.

26 D. Deplanche, 'Le jeu du "Fort-Da", ou l'incidence du symbolique sur le sujet', Paris, *Les feuillets du Courtil*, 2000, p. 10.

27 G. Cullere-Crespin, *L'épopée symbolique du nouveau-né*, op. cit. pp. 43–4.

28 J. Bergès, G. Balbo, *Psychose, autisme et défaillance cognitive chez l'enfant*, op. cit. 2010, pp. 17–18.

29 G. Cullere-Crespin, *L'épopée symbolique du nouveau-né*, op. cit. pp. 43–6.

30 Ibid. p. 47.

31 D. Deplanche, 'Le jeu du "Fort-Da", ou l'incidence du symbolique sur le sujet', op. cit. p. 10.

32 J. Lacan '*The Four Fundamental Concepts*', op. cit. p. 196.

33 Ibid. p.198.

34 A. Didier-Weill, *Un mystère plus lointain que l'inconscient*, op. cit. p. 16.

35 Ibid. p. 17.

36 S. Freud, '*Jokes and their Relation to the Unconscious*' (1905), Standard Edition 8, p.13.

37 M.-C. Laznik, 'Des psychanalystes qui travaillent en santé publique', op. cit. p. 107.
38 A. Didier-Weill, *Un mystère plus lointain que l'inconscient*, op. cit. p. 17.
39 J. Lacan, *'The Seminar Book 3, The Psychoses'* (1955–6), ed. J.-A. Miller, London, Routledge, 1993, p. 134.
40 P. Malengreau, 'Paroles de familles', op. cit.
41 J.-A. Miller, 'Interpréter l'enfant', op. cit. p. 24.
42 J. Lacan, *'Ecrits'*, op. cit. p. 569.

Chapter 6

The field of touch

Marie Couvert

As promised earlier, I am going to take up the challenge of bringing the dimension of touch into the field of the drive. The legitimacy of doing so is based on the fact that Freud mentioned it, even though he did not produce an exhaustive list of the various partial drives. And while Lacan extended the list by adding the invocatory drive, he did so without any pretension to having made it complete. But above all, this hypothesis occurred to me on the basis of the distinction made by Marie Rose Moro between two types of mothering: the proximal and the distal.[1] She established, in fact, that babies caught up in a distal exchange are more attuned to the scopic, whereas for the others, such as those in African societies, who are not kept at such a distance, the register of the scopic does not appear to be central at all.

The babies in the latter group are by no means outside the field of the drives; it is simply that they have access to it via a different pathway. Indeed, the babies who are caught up in proximal exchanges are almost always carried and cared for through body-to-body experiences with those who fulfil the role of primordial other. So in those cases, it is in the arena of the tactile that we need to locate the drive.

This hypothesis was reinforced by certain clinical situations which gave me food for thought. Certain babies who barely looked at anything at all seemed to me to enter into the encounter with the other by choosing the register of touch in a quite singular way. For these very tiny subjects, the tactile seemed to open up a pathway into the circuit of the drives.

The object of the tactile, namely touch, has the effect of making the real of the body exist for the baby. And yet certain babies will not allow themselves to experience the impact of touch. Quite on the contrary, everything happens as if they had to escape from it. They stiffen up, or go limp, defending themselves with a tonicity that makes it impossible for them to be held. Such babies seem impossible to reconstitute physically; no amount of holding is sufficient to endow them with a bodily envelope. For these babies, there is nothing that can delineate an initial contour or give an impression of a first body image. So how can we make something of the real of the body exist for these babies, who we can say have an extreme sensitivity at the level of the skin?

Héra was one of these babies. Her mother told me how sudden and complicated this baby's arrival into the world had been. Héra was born prematurely, suffering from a foetal disorder which resulted from a rupture of the amniotic sac. Following the birth, and placed on her mother's belly, she choked, and had to be resuscitated. The mother told me that it was she who became anxious about the state of her little daughter, and had to point out to the medical team, who were too busy to notice, that her baby was turning blue. Since then, Héra had presented with hypotonic lower limbs, as well as a vacant stare which her mother had not failed to observe. The baby was then referred to paediatric neurologists and physiotherapists. One of these professionals let slip that the baby might be at risk of autism. That was enough to throw the mother into a state of boundless anxiety. At just three weeks, Héra found herself stuck in this diagnosis, the prisoner of a remark that should never have been made. Today we know that external influences have the power to reverse certain symptoms, and prior to the age of one year a baby presenting with a withdrawn state is particularly susceptible to such intervention.

She was three months old when she came to see me with her mother. Héra had eyes only for the ceiling. "I love everything that's up in the air . . .", said the defeated mother, speaking on behalf of her daughter. Héra also found it impossible to let herself be cuddled, and for weeks on end I never saw her being held. Indeed, her hypotonia made her like a slippery eel when anyone tried to pick her up. Certainly, like all babies, Héra was responsive to the prosody of motherese; her eyes would move away from the ceiling and stare into mine when she heard me. This was an important indicator, and I did not neglect to share it with her mother. However, as the sessions went on, I became quite depressed because I felt I had to start from scratch each time. Héra never seemed to recognise me. The things she chose to latch on to and focus on were invariably the same: the light and the ceiling. Her mother, who was no fool, said with an air of contrition, "Those are her friends: the ceiling and the light."

It was working with the body and touching the body that enabled Héra to truly look at me and eventually to be held. It was the tactile object that became the agent through which the baby could discover her own bodily envelope, an initial contour which both put together and delimited what was 'her'. I decided to touch her in a way that was almost ethereal. Using a feather, I stroked the upper surfaces of her tiny feet, and then beneath the arches. Her response was immediate: she looked towards her feet and followed the gentle motions I was making with the feather with intense interest. So she had a foot, and soon she would have two! This allowed her to grab hold of them. She took her little feet in her hands, joining hands to feet vertically. For the first time, Héra was trying things out which would unify her and finally give her a bodily axis. Her eyes followed almost immediately. I was still holding the feather with my finger-tips, stroking her little cheeks, her forehead, the contours of her face, and her eyes looked deep into mine. Héra had allowed herself to be affected by the tactile, and soon I was glad to see the drive take hold of her.

This is what she did: she grabbed the feather, gently moved it to her face, and stroked her own cheek. Then, looking deeply into my eyes, she held out her hand to my face, and I felt my cheek being stroked by the feather she was still holding. I was overcome with emotion, all the more so when I saw her turn towards her mother, snuggling into her arms and running the feather over her face. From that day on, Héra recognised me and smiled radiantly each time we met. So in her case it was a gentle touch, light as a feather, which was the agent of the initial inscription of the drive. It marked her body, enabling it to exist and be present for her; and this allowed her to make a primary differentiation between herself and an other. She then grasped the feather herself, and this act opened up the space for a desire to make the other exist for her. That is how the sense of touch, a tactile object, had the power to enable Héra to enter into the circuits of the drive.

But that is not all; it also established that the field of the tactile has all the characteristics of the partial drives and their montage.

Characteristics of the tactile register

The *object* of the tactile register, as we have just seen, brings into play the field of touch, the closest relation to the other. The newborn baby, in order to be fed, looked at and spoken to, is always picked up and held. "The child's relation of familiarity with an object is recognised initially through touch, through fingering, through the touch with which he or she invests it."[2] Touching, of course, implies movement. Jean-Marie Forget, in *Les enjeux des pulsions*, had already raised motricity to the level of a drive.[3] But a close reading introduces us to the grammar of the drives, which follows a trajectory with three times, and is now familiar to us.[4]

On the other hand, the object of the tactile, while emerging from movement, has the particularity of being resolutely aimed at the other. It is almost innate in its structure, because touching includes being touched. And because of the immaturity of small babies, they are constantly being touched, their bodies are always doubled with that of an other. This was Winnicott's valuable discovery regarding the sense of touch, which he developed in his concepts of *holding* and *handling*.[5]

Holding and the touch involved in it allow the baby to experiment with a contour, points of contact and support, rhythmicity, the alternation of presence and absence of the other. Babies may affirm whether or not they are present by snuggling in the mother's arms, by allowing themselves to be stroked and rocked; or on the contrary, when touch becomes unbearable to them, and being picked up and held upsets them to the extent that they cannot be soothed. They may even activate touch and be its agent, by grasping the fingers of the caregiver. So, far from proceeding from a need, we can see that touch is a powerful channel for the drive.

As for the *source*, it comes into play in the envelope of the skin. Freud mentioned early on that the skin has the characteristic of being excitable, and evokes "a special intensification of a kind of susceptibility to stimulus" that has to be attributed to it.[6] We are indebted to Didier Anzieu for having emphasised the importance of the skin in the constitution of the ego.[7] More recently, work by André Bullinger has taught us that the skin constitutes the outermost envelope, and the one that is sought in the encounter with the other.[8] It also covers the muscular envelope and the percussion instrument constituted by the skeleton. Following on from Anzieu and his concept of the 'skin-ego', Bullinger gave us the concepts of the 'muscle-ego' and the 'bone-ego'. Each of these layers – bone, muscle, skin – is one of the most archaic supports of the baby and constitutes a key factor in the tactile encounter with the other. Some babies who are at risk of autism cannot be reached unless they are summoned by beating rhythmically on their skeleton, while a more peripheral touch will disturb them acutely. Others seem to seek muscular relaxation through a touch that invites flexing. We can account for this through the dimension of sexuality that circulates via the envelope of the skin. Indeed, the skin, which opens up the register of touch, certainly has the edge-like structure that is characteristic of the erogenous zones. It is a porous envelope which allows babies to feel an initial difference between their interior and their exterior. It is the edge which both delimits and separates what is the baby from what is the other.

We can see that "this formation of a skin-container is so closely bound up with sexuality".[9] It is also a valuable source of information, which it filters and receives with an extraordinary degree of sensitivity. For example, the skin can distinguish jerky, abrupt touches from gentle strokes, hands which brush accidentally against it from those which caress, hands that massage from those that prod, those that soothe and calm, but also those that annoy, that rub too hard, that hurt . . . In response, the baby may tense up, the muscular envelope becomes rigid and stiff, or else he or she may relax, the muscles becoming more supple; the child becomes slack and calm. The skin colour may become heightened or may become cyanotic; it can form a texture which makes it less porous, even eczematous and weeping, or else it can be smooth and have a delicious smell. Fundamentally, we can say that the envelope of the skin is a surface which can be written upon. In doing so, the baby constructs a sort of psychical identity card of the person who touches him or her; but above all, the skin experiences pleasure and unpleasure. Pleasure is the surplus value at play in satisfaction, and that is its only aim.

Thus the *aim* of the drive in the tactile register is nothing other than the satisfaction which generally proceeds from an experience of pleasure linked most often to the soothing aspect of touch. However, certain other types of experiences of excitation such as tickling are not without an element of pleasure and can also lead to satisfaction. In addition, many babies show that they can also satisfy themselves with something that is really not satisfying, by seeking out tactile experiences that are actually sources of unpleasure. In other words, tactile satisfaction is multifarious and may take the chosen pathway to pleasure, or may take the diversions leading to unpleasure. From this perspective, satisfaction in the register of the tactile drive illustrates perfectly the demand of the drive and its failures, because it obliges us to consider pleasure without departing from the Freudian dimension of a "beyond the pleasure principle".

As for Freud's *pressure*, which he taught us is a constant force, we know that it is a way of making us understand that the pressure of the drive is opposed to the idea of a single definitive satisfaction. From this point of view, we would need to question whether the sense of touch, once it has been satisfied, would desert us all together, or leave us completely indifferent. It would seem, rather, that the sense of touch is a prelude which is always there to open the doorways of desire. It is so true that touch penetrates us at every age, in a way that is both imperious and yet also experienced anew each time, when it comes to love. It is also the ultimate form of pleasure and presence when we are face to face with the most radical experience of life, when we are at the point of dying. We could say, then, that there is something insistent mediated by the sense of touch, and it is through this very insistence that the drive can be grasped, as Lacan showed us.

The tactile drive: setting up the circuit

If we are to include the tactile alongside the other drives, we need to show how it is established in the drive circuit, with its three constituent times. The grammatical rules of the drives involve three times:

- *In the first active time, touching with the palm of the hand*, which can be observed in newborn babies in their capacity to grasp an object. Who has not had the unsettling experience of a baby barely out of the womb squeezing the finger of the adult who has come to stroke the tiny hand? This gripping of the other not only has the effect of soothing the baby, but also, according to Brazelton, constitutes neonatal relational competence, with the power to promote a parent to the rank of mother or father.[10]
- *We then find a second reflexive time; babies now play at catching hold of their own hands or feet.* In doing this, babies give themselves an object to hang on to or grasp, and this is not without a dimension of autoerotism But that is not all; we can see that this experience of grabbing hold of the babies' own body constitutes part of the construction of the lateral and vertical axes of development which enable them to apprehend the space in which they will now be able to evolve.

- *Finally, in the third time of passivisation, babies try to make themselves touched.* Newborns may experiment very early on with this power of action which they exert over others. While they are still immature, incapable of moving from one place to another or articulating a demand, they nonetheless, in the strength of their screaming, have the means to provoke a degree of concern in whoever occupies the place of the primordial other; and this will make the latter move from one place to another, lean over the cradle, and eventually pick them up and rock them in their arms. Over the course of a few months, the third stage of 'making oneself touched' will undergo a number of modifications. We may watch it transform and develop into other forms of touch, such as games of tickling, so relished by both babies and their parents.

So *touching, touching oneself and making oneself touched* constitute the three grammatical stages of the tactile register. But as with any grammatical construction, there are exceptions to the rule; and in the field we are concerned with, there can also be failures.

I would now like to focus on these failures in the drive circuit, because they are what have taught me how to use the register of touch both as a compass and as an operator of the drives.

Failure of the first time: touching

The activation of the first stage usually manifests itself in a healthy baby through the capacity to grasp hold of things. It is generally agreed that this capacity is a reflex activity. From that point of view, it would be of little interest to us and would not qualify for the status of partial drive. As we shall see, however, some babies are capable of gripping and grasping in a more deliberate way.

This was the case with Léa, a five-month-old baby, who encouraged me to take up the challenge of enabling her to enter into the dimension of the tactile in the field of the drives.

She was a baby who did not invest the more usual registers of the drives. In the field of orality, she never demanded anything, but would allow herself to be bottle-fed without so much as blinking. In the scopic field, she had chosen neither to look nor to allow herself to be looked at by those who tried to do so. She would turn her head away, frowning, and refuse to become involved in any interaction.

In the register of invocation, she had decided not to hear anything. Léa did not seem to engage in any register, and at first sight she seemed no more inclined to allow herself to be reached through touch.

Although all babies show the capacity to grip, Léa, aged almost five months, never took hold of or grasped anything. The mobility and tonus of her fingers showed such a degree of ankylosis that she was completely unable to grasp anything, or later to grab hold of an object. It was only with a real effort, a disconcerting slowness, and a mobility that she seemed to have summoned against her will, that her hand would move with enormous difficulty towards a rattle, only to touch it weakly and then stop all together. There was no prehensile movement, and her touch was absolutely minimal: that was her signature. Being touched by somebody else was similarly unbearable for her. If I invited her to give me her hand to say hello, she would always refuse to do so; I would have to go to try to pick her up, and almost always Léa would avoid me with an unequivocal gesture of withdrawal.

And yet reading more closely what Léa was showing us allowed me to wonder whether this baby might be able to use the tactile register as an unusual psychical position. The only touch that Léa seemed to seek out, and would refuse to let go of, was that of her mother. The pair clung together so closely that it was impossible to know whether it was Léa who was positioning herself as a 'suckering' object on her mother, or the mother who was vampirising the child. One thing was certain: on close observation, there was nothing at all that could be classified as a gripping motion in this clinging together.

Léa succeeded in the project of touching her mother, but in an absolutely passive way. It allowed her to be touched without ever having to make the effort to touch. It was activity that this baby was energetically trying to avoid. In this first stage of activity, Léa was like a magnet, and seemed to gain satisfaction exclusively from sticking herself to the other. But nothing took place between them, not a single movement, not the slightest playfulness, not a word, absolutely nothing. One evening, when the mother was lying on the sofa in the unit, Léa was stretched out on her, rather like a brooch ornamenting her mother's chest. Both mother and daughter appeared to me to be in a state of boundless ecstasy. It was as if the sexuality which characterises the partial drives were saturated with a jouissance fed by the death drive. Witnessing this tactile adhesion, I had become a spectator of the asphyxiation of the drives between mother and daughter.

Failure of the second time: touching oneself

Léa did not engage in the second time either, where ordinary babies grasp their own hands and feet, finding pleasure in taking hold of parts of their own body as objects to grip. We can observe very tiny babies joining their hands together over their mouth or eyes, sweeping them across the lateral space. A little later, they grab hold of their own feet, and begin to execute asymmetrical manoeuvres, taking the right foot in the left hand and vice versa. By activating these points of juncture, babies are experimenting in their own ways with versions of holding which resemble, or take the place of, the maternal container.

At this stage, everything occurs as though babies, by grasping parts of their own body, were operating a displacement of satisfaction, which certainly gives them a certain pleasure. As Geneviève Haag pointed out, "the hand which can set about manipulating things is first of all an autoerotic hand, and the foot which will eventually walk is first of all an autoerotic foot".[11] But that is not all; the activity between the left and the right and the upper and lower parts of the body, participates in the construction of a bodily axis in the search for balance and bearing which, in my view, prefigures a pre-specular grasp of a body that is the baby's own, and is separate from that of the other.

But there was no trace of this in Léa. Her body was of no interest to her. It seemed she had neither hands nor feet. And besides, why would she need them, since her mother's hands and feet were constantly at her disposal to carry her and move her around? Stuck to her mother like a magnet, she moved at the mother's whim, only coming and going when she did, and never demanded anything other than to remain stuck to her. So it seemed that her mother's body was joined to hers, like a prosthesis. Léa only existed by proxy. For her, the displacement of satisfaction was impossible.

On the other hand, it was impossible to deny that there was indeed some satisfaction caught up in this renunciation of her own existence.

What position can an analyst take up when he or she witnesses 'live' the non-advent of the subject or a subject who keeps failing to appear? Certainly, an analyst cannot just do nothing. At least I was armed with a degree of interpretative knowledge. The failure of the first two stages had taught me enough about Léa's position. From being a magnetic object, she was now well on the way to becoming an incorporated object. But I could not count on her mother to dislodge her from that position. Barely 19 years old, she had also been the object of her own mother. In order to defend herself, she had constructed a carapace of obesity, to an exceptionally morbid degree. In this way she existed purely by absorbing. So I found myself confronted with a mother who did not realise she was an ogress, and a baby who demanded nothing but to be swallowed whole by her.

My first interpretation was therefore based on the necessity for the drives to get moving, through the introduction of any form of third term: I proffered myself as a substitutive object, and eroticised the most insignificant rattle. I tried to create a small distance between them, and suggested putting Léa down on the play mat; down on all fours, I went for it with my most beautiful prosody. Running out of ideas, I suggested that we should wait a bit, thinking that it might be possible to overcome Léa's imperious demand to always be returned to clamp herself to the maternal bosom.

I had it all wrong. Léa did not want anything, absolutely nothing, other than to return like a limpet to her mother's adipose body. To every suggestion I made, Léa said "No". By this time she was fully capable of howling endlessly, without pausing for breath; she would stare at me with her dark eyes and show me her teeth, which were now numerous. I was crushed. This baby had such power, such atrocious determination, wanting nothing other than her mother. It took me some time to overcome my own resistance, and to accept that it was precisely this power that I needed to acknowledge. Indeed, I had wanted to get Léa engaged in the circuit of the drives, without realising that she was already involved in it with all her might. I could now see that she was extraordinarily alive, precisely at the point where she gave the impression that she was far from being so.

So I altered my approach, guided by the logic of the third time of the drive circuit.

Failure/success of the third time: making oneself touched

Should we speak of failure or success of the third time in Léa's case?

If we focus on what was most unusual about this baby, and which made her unclassifiable, there was no evidence that the third time had not been successfully reached.

As we know, this is the stage of "making oneself done to", where babies actively lend themselves to being the object of a satisfaction provoked in the other. In doing this, we also know that it does not occur without something of the subject being produced. How was it that I had not noticed that Léa actually excelled in terms of the third stage? Better and earlier than many other babies, she had found out how to arouse the pleasure her mother was expecting from her. We could even wonder if this baby had entered into the circuit of the drives via the third stage. Indeed, by doing everything to make her mother her exclusive object of satisfaction, Léa eminently proved her own subjectivity, at the same time as creating subjectivity in her mother, by assuring her that she was the only one able to satisfy her.

This is how Léa taught me, because one had to acknowledge that the way she had inscribed herself in the third stage displayed a certain know-how in dealing with the one who was in the position of her primordial other.

The mother in turn lost no opportunity to tell her daughter that she might show interest in something else: Take this pretty rattle! Stay there on the mat! Look at what Madame Couvert is showing you! The mother said to her very gently, "You can do it, you know, Léa . . .". And yet something in her voice did not really invite the baby to do it. On the other hand, her smile, when Léa ultimately did not give up on wanting her and her alone, was absolutely radiant, and seemed to take over her entire face. This baby had discovered how to make her into a perfectly satisfied and fulfilled mother. So I had to work with her invention, even if Léa paid a heavy toll for having activated this "making oneself touched all the time"; she was lagging several months behind on almost all the Bayley test items,[12] showing significant signs of inversion and withdrawal, and had an alarming score for depression on the ADBB[13] scale, because the emerging subject was completely alienated.

This is precisely where the failure had occurred but it was also in the production of a subject so peculiarly rebellious against anyone other than her mother that there was an opportunity for action. I therefore stopped desiring, I gave up making any sort of interpretation imbued with meaning. On the other hand, I tried to stay as close as possible to what was actually going on between Léa and her mother and what they were creating. And I used the third time of the circuit of the drive as a lever.

Making use of the third time

The first step was to recognise the extent to which the third time was working for Léa.

Whenever Léa noticed her mother, her first intention was to be 'picked up', without ever having to ask. All it needed was for them to see each other, and Léa would find herself flying into the air and landing on her mother's belly. If the mother put Léa down, a little cry was all that was needed to bring the baby back onto this extraordinary lap which had no hollows, but consisted of a number of adipose cushions piled one on top of the other.

During the sessions, Léa would always cling to her mother's arms, and if they came face to face it was only at the price of a twisting which put the child into a position of opisthotonus, the lower part of her body stuck to her mother's, and the upper part almost completely slack. When she had her back to her mother, it was the opposite: all the upper part of her body seemed to be trying to push itself into the mother's flesh, as if she had to recover at all costs the position she had lost by being carried face-to-face. Léa would rub her head and the upper part of her back against her mother's bosom, with the result that the mother would smile, both embarrassed and delighted. I emphasised how totally satisfied the mother and baby were with each other. "Look how right you are for each other!" I said, "Léa loves to be in your arms more than anything else, and you love having her in your arms more than anything else."

Basically, I was trying to work with this symptomatic invention I had observed, this capacity to 'stick together' that animated both mother and daughter. My look had no function other than to register and acknowledge what was going on between the two of them.

At this point I was working in the opposite direction to the rest of the team, who quite rightly considered this sticking together to be nothing other than eminently pathological. On the contrary, I made sure that I showed Léa as much as I could how important I thought it was that she, in her mother's arms, was finding pleasure as well as providing her mother with pleasure. This is what signals the third time of the circuit of the drives.

This did not fail to have an effect: using the symptom as something with the effect of a signature, something remarkable, unclassifiable, I deciphered that this symptomatic behaviour between Léa and her mother was based on a very precise object of the drive: *touch*, and that in this touch, the modality of sticking together was the mark of the engagement of the drive. In a certain way, I was giving this extreme sticking together the status of a creation which was part of a new subjective structure.

Now we shall see that this new subjective structure had its own effects.

From here on, Léa would come up with new forms of sticking together. In a completely new way, she started to stick to her mother differently: climbing up her body, snuggling into her, climbing over her, while clinging on to her. One day she even went so far as to let herself slide down her; with her back against her mother, who was sitting on the floor, Léa allowed herself to slide gently down as far as her leg, and from her leg, right down to the floor. Echoing her sliding from her mother's soft body to the hard floor of my consulting room, I simply said, "Bang!".

Léa, amazed, briefly burst out laughing, and then she wanted to do it all over again. Bang, Bang, Bang, Bang, just four letters, showing the power of a single syllable as an interpretation. Bang: that encapsulated all the pleasure Léa found, mediated by the touch of the hard floor, in the manifestation, the making present of something that for the first time could have the effect of an Other for her.

In doing this, the little 'speaking being' Léa was no longer simply a 'sticking being', because now she was on the way to becoming a 'moving being'. Still using the same model of sticking, which seemed to entail an unshakeable loyalty to her mother, she began to move – but never without her mother!

So when she was on the point of crawling, her mother had to do the same. Léa was sitting in the corridor that led to my consulting room, but instead of launching herself forward, she seemed to be riveted to the floor, incapable of unsticking herself.

A story came back to me from a children's book[14] about Madame K. Madame K was a big fat lady who never did anything, and had nothing apart from an old husband. That is, until the day she found a baby bird that had fallen out of the nest. After she had nursed it, and fed it by hunting day and night for tiny insects, she realised that it had become grown, and decided that it was ready to fly away. But nothing happened: the bird stayed on a branch, and would not leave her. So, without hesitation, Madame K decided she had to show it what to do, climbed the tree, heavy as she was, and threw herself off the highest branch . . . and the bird followed suit. So I said to the mother, "Madame, without you we won't get there." And the mother, following my example, went down on all fours, and we crawled along the corridors, watched by colleagues who gave us encouraging looks. That is what decided and delighted Léa. The corridor became an annexe to my consulting room, a kind of umbilical cord between myself and Léa's mother, where our long sessions could now take place.

Léa now began to use intermediate spaces. I joined in her games, suggesting various supporting structures for her to stick to; sessions now took place on mats upon which she would allow herself to be carried from one place to another, and which went back and forth between her mother and myself. Léa tried out variants of the going-and-coming back game, carried by a person who could now be someone other than her mother.

This enabled her to revisit the other times of the tactile register. In the corridors, she would stop, turn round and grab hold of her mother, so that the latter would support her so she could walk. She was showing me that she could now actively engage with the first time of the drive.

A little later, she amazed me by showing me a mirror stage that was completely imbued with the second stage of the drive circuit. During one session, she clambered over the mats that had been used to carry her and move her around, to reach the big mirror just beyond them. Léa hoisted herself up so she could stick to the mirror, and then, with a great and sustained effort, she began to touch the image of her body with her hands and with her mouth, all the while looking at us in delight.

Finally, she achieved a real *tour de force* by revisiting the third stage of the tactile drive in a way that almost metaphorically 'made herself touching'.

It was our last session, and I was going over all the work we had done with her and her mother. I spoke about her first movements, and I stopped on the effect of the word "Bang!" In front of the mirror, Léa replayed the scene, letting herself slide down from her mother's lap onto the hard floor once again, and showing off with peals of laughter. She looked at us, and I said, "Little rascal, you know how to be a little rascal now, don't you?" And then I took a risk: "Do you want to say 'rascal'? Can you say 'rascal' for Madame Couvert?" And Léa, who was only 16 months old, looked me straight in the eye with a big toothy smile, and said, "Rascal", loud and clear. This little girl, who only had two words in her active vocabulary, "Baby"and "Bye-bye", had succeeded in provoking in both her mother and myself an extraordinary degree of amazement and pleasure.[15] And that is how Léa, who had been an 'untouchable' baby for so long, showed us that she knew how to make herself into an extremely 'touching' little girl.

Notes

1 M.R. Moro, *Enfants d'ici venus d'ailleurs,* Paris, La Découverte, 2002.
2 J. Bergès, G. Balbo, *Psychose, autisme et défaillance cognitive chez l'enfant,* op. cit. p. 31.
3 J.M. Forget, *Les enjeux des pulsions,* op. cit. pp. 82–102.
4 Jean Marie Forget, in the distinction he makes between the three grammatical voices, notes the active voice, "I move", I twitch/kick; passive, "I am moved", I am manipulated; and reflexive, "I make myself moved". So if we are to respect the grammar of the drive, the first stage, that of activity, should be turned towards the object; the second stage should be translated by: "I move a part of my own body, my hand, my fingers, my feet"; and the third stage, that of passivity, which corresponds to the passivisation of the subject, would then involve the register where the baby him or herself acts in a reflexive way: "I make myself moved". Jean Marie Forget himself does not omit to point out other difficulties: for example, the source

of this motor drive does not follow a circuit of reversion and its constancy, seems difficult to explain. See *Les enjeux des pulsions*, op. cit. p. 95.

5 D.W. Winnicott, 'Communication Between Infant and Mother, and Mother and Infant, Compared and Contrasted' (1968), in Clare Winnicott et al., eds, *Babies and their Mothers*, Reading, MA, Addison-Wesley, 1987, pp. 89–103.

6 S. Freud, *Three Essays*, op. cit. p. 201.

7 D. Anzieu, *Le Moi-peau*, Paris, Dunod, 1995.

8 A. Bullinger, *Le développement sensori-moteur de l'enfant et ses avatars*, Toulouse, érès, 2004.

9 G. Haag, "Sexualité orale et moi corporel", *Topique*, No. 87, *Les resurgences de l'archaïque*, 2004, p. 15.

10 T. B. Brazelton, J. K. Nugent, *NBAS, Neonatal Behavioral Assessment Scale*, op. cit.

11 G. Haag, 'Sexualité orale et moi corporel', op. cit. p. 23.

12 The Bayley Test is a developmental test for babies aged 1–42 months. Applied in a clinical setting, it is more discriminating than the Brunet-Lézine Test, particularly in that it differentiates between understanding and expression where language is concerned. This is why it is administered in conjunction with the Brunet-Lézine Test in our unit.

13 Alarm, distress, baby; this is a scale which sets out to assess the level of distress in a baby in terms of withdrawal. It is administered in the unit by nursery nurses when a baby continues to present signs of withdrawal in spite of psychotherapeutic work and other interventions. See A. Guedeney, 'L'échelle ADBB: intérêt en recherche et en clinique de l'évaluation du comportement de retrait relationnel du jeune enfant', *Médecine et enfance*, June 2004, pp. 367–71.

14 W. Erlbruch, *Remue-ménage chez Madame K*, Paris, Milan, 1995.

15 I could have remained in the register of a signifying interpretation, taking the link the two signifiers "baby" and "bye-bye", which were articulated so precociously, as an expression of a movement of separation. But this would have left out the desire of the mother, which always drew Léa back to her so powerfully within this modality of sticking together.

Conclusion

Marie Couvert

There are several possible answers to the question of what it is that we do when we work clinically with babies: we delineate the different registers that need to be put in place in the young baby; we use these registers as compasses to guide ourselves within a structural framework; and we use these guiding principles to find a direction in our clinical work.

We still have to pinpoint the operators responsible for inscribing the circuits of the drives in order to bring about a transformation in the very young subject.

From among these operators, I would isolate three: the sexual, jouissance and the interweaving of the drives.

The sexual, yes, because without the engagement of the sexual, there is no drive! A film about David Lynch, *The Art Life*, illustrates this very well.[1] We see the cineaste at work, and then something strange appears in the image. The camera is permanently fixed on his hands, and we see nothing but close-ups of them. They never stop cutting, splicing, fiddling with small objects, spreading things out, painting, modelling textures. The film shows hands and fingers frenetically flying about and making things. There is something very alive in these hands, something urgent and insistent, which echoes the things his father encouraged him to make as a child. Something was transmitted, which meant that the subject had it in his very hands! That is where the sexual slips in, that it where we can discern it. Without it, Lynch would not have been the person he is. In a certain way, Lynch could only be Lynch thanks to the actions of his hands. And it is the necessity of the engagement of the sexual that we need to look for when we work clinically with babies. This does not mean introducing something that is not there already. Rather it means we must know how to grasp it. Grasping the sexual, it seems to me, is exactly that 'thing' that has agency. And that thing can always be spotted at the point where it insists.

Jouissance is the compass of the transference. It is set going once there is a supposition of an Other, whether this occurs on the side of the baby or of the mother or the analyst. If we can agree to hypothesise that there is a subject in the newborn baby, then we can also suppose that there is an Other for him or her. "This means that we have to suppose the existence of a big Other for each of them, mother and child",[2] as Bergès put it. When a mother addresses her baby, when she speaks to him or her and anxiously awaits a response, she lends a power to the child. And this crazy power that she attributes to the child tears him or her from a position as object, and "propels him or her out of the place of the Thing".[3] This extraordinary investment creates something for the mother as much as for the baby. And this is exactly what the analyst puts in place at the first encounter with an analysand. Lacan was well aware of this when he noted, "the analyst says to whoever is about to begin – 'Away you go, say whatever, it will be marvelous'".[4] That is what creates a subject and calls something of the Other into being. "This big Other corresponds to a hypothesis made by the other, something one can credit him or her with, whether it is the mother for the child or the child for the mother",[5] and the same goes for the analyst. Whenever a newborn baby is passionately invested, a mother madly in love with her child, an analyst intensely full of supposition on behalf of an analysand, something always happens. We then see babies rounding out their lips, the little tongue moving, trying to find a way to make the sound which is so longed for. But beyond the sound, what is produced is the jouissance anticipated on the side of the other. This primordial jouissance is fundamental because it signals the putting into place of what we can call an 'in between'. In other words, what emerges is something that is constructed between the baby and the mother or analyst. From that moment on we can be sure that the Other is in circulation. For those who work clinically with very young babies, daring to involve jouissance – obviously provided that it is barred – proceeds from an *analytic act*.

When, in spite of myself, I said, "Stop!" to Victor, when I kissed Marianne, when I swung Héra gently up in the air over and over again, or when I said the word "Rascal!" to Léa, which she so much wanted to hear, all of these were doubtless acts of this nature.

The interweaving of the drives was already observed by Freud, when he considered muscular activity. He also noted that the pleasure connected with muscular tension is reinforced by the excitation caused by skin contact.[6] But it was Jean Bergès who identified the action of this reinforcement as that which causes the inscription of the drives. In other words, in order for inscription to take place, there needs to be an interweaving of the drives. If we explore this further on the basis of the registers of the drives, we shall then see that the fields of the drives cannot be entirely isolated from one another. When ordinary babies latch on to the breast during the first stage of orality, they also hear the mother's words, read the mother's lips, touch her skin . . . The oral, the invocatory, the scopic and the tactile are forever being interwoven. "All of that constitutes a kind of motor",[7] as Bergès puts it. By this we should understand that the interweaving of the drives is a motor in the operation of the inscription of the drives. And it is precisely at the point that the drives are interwoven that babies 'at risk' seem to experience difficulty or withdraw. They are thus deprived of this motor of inscription. When these babies are feeding, you can see them looking away, or else they do not latch on, and their tiny hands just hang loosely; and if you call out to them, they do not initiate any movement. So it is not sufficient to assume that the circuit of the drives can be set in motion through a single register; it is necessary to activate whatever will allow the different registers to become intertwined. This reinforcing effect is what we need to bear in mind when we work with babies, because interweaving is a decisive factor.

Introducing the sexual, daring to bring in jouissance through the supposition of the Other, activating the interweaving of the drives: these are what constitute the agencies of the drives.

And it is up to us to make use of them when we work clinically with very young babies.

Notes

1   *David Lynch: The Art Life*, documentary directed by Jon Nguyen and Rick Barnes.
2   J. Bergès, G. Balbo, *Psychose, autism et défaillance cognitive chez l'enfant*, op. cit. p. 10.
3   Ibid. p. 9.
4   J. Lacan, '*The Other Side of Psychoanalysis*', op. cit. p. 52.
5   J. Bergès, G. Balbo, *Psychose, autisme et défaillance cognitive chez l'enfant*, op. cit. p. 13.
6   S. Freud, *Three Essays*, op. cit. p. 203.
7   J. Bergès, G. Balbo, *L'enfant et la psychanalyse*, op. cit. 1994.

For Product Safety Concerns and Information please contact our EU
representative GPSR@taylorandfrancis.com
Taylor & Francis Verlag GmbH, Kaufingerstraße 24, 80331 München, Germany